Secrets
of a
Millionaire Landlord

MAXIMIZE PROFITS AND MINIMIZE HASSLES

Secrets of a

MILLIONAIRE LANDLORD

ROBERT SHEMIN, ESQ.

Dearborn™
Trade Publishing
A **Kaplan Professional** Company

This publication is designed to provide accurate and authoritative information in regard to the subject matter covered. It is sold with the understanding that the publisher is not engaged in rendering legal, accounting, or other professional service. If legal advice or other expert assistance is required, the services of a competent professional person should be sought.

Acquisitions Editor: Mary B. Good
Senior Managing Editor: Jack Kiburz
Interior Design: Lucy Jenkins
Cover Design: Design Alliance, Inc.
Typesetting: Elizabeth Pitts

© 2002 by Dearborn Financial Publishing, Inc.

Published by Dearborn Trade Publishing, a Kaplan Professional Company

Printed in the United States of America

02 03 04 10 9 8 7 6 5 4 3

Library of Congress Cataloging-in-Publication Data

Shemin, Robert, 1963-
    Secrets of a millionaire landlord / Robert Shemin.
        p.   cm.
    Includes index.
    ISBN 0-7931-4825-1 (pbk.)
    1. Real estate management—United States. 2. Rental housing—United
States—Management. 3. Landlord and tenant—United States. 4. Real
estate investment—United States. 5. Rental housing—United
States—Forms.   I. Title.
  HD1394.5.U6 S5   2001
  333.33′8′068—dc21

                                                    2001004359

ACKNOWLEDGMENTS

Thank you, all of my tenants, for teaching me what to do and what not to do.

A special thanks to Kevin Machon of Machon Properties, and to Melissa, for doing such a good job.

This book would not have been possible without the editorial help of Steve Trinward and Barbara McNichol. Also, I am thankful for all of the help, support, and patience from Dearborn Trade Publishing, especially from Mary B. Good.

Janie, you made finishing this book so much fun.

To Alexander, thank you for your patience. Know that all I do, I do for you!

CONTENTS

The Landlord's Journey Begins

The man with a new idea is a crank until the idea succeeds.

–Mark Twain

My name is Robert Shemin. I started in real estate at the age of 27. I had a full-time job and, like 80 percent of Americans, dreaded going to work on Monday morning. Possibly like you, I always had an idea in mind: I want to stop working for somebody else; I want to start my own business. I had no idea what I wanted to do, although I was certain I did not want to get into real estate. I worked in financial consulting and I was paid and treated well. But I still wanted my own business.

One day, I was invited into an older couple's home in Madison, Tennessee—the nicest couple in the world. I stopped in for about 15 to 20 minutes, talked to them, and had almost concluded they didn't match my firm's financial portfolio. They had a dumpy little office and a business called American Property Improvements. I told them, "Well, it's obvious you don't have enough money for our firm to help you out. By the way, what do you do for a living?"

This older gentleman, who had never even graduated from high school, replied, "I buy houses, I renovate them, and I rent them out."

"Well, that is a neat business. How does it work?" I asked.

"Come over here, sonny. Let me show you something," he replied. He opened a huge accounting book and showed me that he had 96 properties, all paid for. The business had about $65,000 a month coming in, and he and his wife had just taken a six-month vacation.

All of a sudden, young, cocksure Robert—who thought he had a good job and no interest in real estate—got very interested in real estate. I decided to interview 200 real estate investors and 200 tenants in low-, moderate-, and high-income brackets. I did extensive research, as if I were investigating any other kind of business. I learned about the industry, the challenges, and the competition. And I discovered many interesting facts in a short period of time.

The first thing I learned about tenants was this: Most believe they are not treated very well. They dislike their landlords, pay their rent late, and don't care for their surroundings. But to me, this all spelled "big opportunity." Finding a business that is unprofessional and unsophisticated, in which most of the customers are treated poorly, can be lucrative if you look at the history of businesses over time. You see, if you have a business in which customers are already happy, there isn't much room to do better, make more money, or be the best provider. But in landlording today, you can elevate the business to a professional level. That's where the opportunity lies.

I know of a gentleman who realized that a lot of store operators treated their customers poorly. Customers could not easily locate things in the stores, and no one would help them do so. So he thought, "Maybe I can open a store and treat customers well, give good value, and provide a clean environment." He did all of these things—and consequently, Sam Walton did extremely well for himself. He built a small operation called Wal-Mart, in Arkansas, into a nationwide retailing success.

I realized that a big part of a workable plan includes treating tenants like valued customers. If I could buy properties where tenants were used to receiving poor treatment, paint the structures, and start treating them well, they would stay longer—maybe even pay their rent on time.

I believe this principle holds true today: If you are a professional landlord who treats people well, you have little competition, because 85 percent of tenants have complaints about their landlords.

Real estate investors are among the most optimistic groups in the world, expecting everything to run smoothly month after month. But some have bad months when money doesn't come in. If notes to repay loans get called in during lean months, these investors may have to declare bankruptcy.

When I interviewed 200 landlords and investors, I found that, although some had done well, about 80 percent had gone bankrupt. Why? They borrowed too much money against their properties, thus overleveraging them. They often got short-term notes that came due for repayment within a year or two. The payment deadline caught them at a time when cash flow was low and forced them into a squeeze. That's why I recommend that you get long-term notes, which may allow you to ride the waves of real estate cycles and avoid bankruptcy.

After conducting my survey of tenants, investors, and landlords—and uncovering lots of problems—I still decided to take the plunge into this ocean of opportunity. Here was my plan. I would find a duplex and mortgage it, borrowing $40,000 for 15 years at 8 to 9 percent. My payment would be about $350 a month, with some give-and-take for taxes and insurance. I could then rent each unit for about $400 a month. If I owned the duplex for 15 years, I would use the rent to cover my debt, including interest, and have a paid-off property worth at least $50,000. Then, if I could buy ten similar properties, I would have half a million dollars in property after 15 years (10 × $50,000 = $500,000). I calculated all this without factoring in a real estate market appreciation. Then I set my plan in motion by buying a brick duplex in a low- to middle-class, moderate-income neighborhood of a mid-sized city.

Not long after I started, I began thinking that 15 or 18 properties would bring in about a million dollars. Now, about what other business can you say after only 15 years: "Congratulations! Here is my retirement. Instead of a gold watch, an engraved pen, or a layoff, I get a million dollars of paid-off property!" That got me hooked.

Thus began my journey into the wonderful world of landlording. Has it been smooth sailing? No. Have I learned a lot? Definitely. That's why I've written this book—so *your* big opportunity can be as hassle-free and lucrative as possible.

CHAPTER 1

Why Landlording?

Some people approach their jobs like a mosquito in a nudist camp—they see lots of opportunity but can't decide where to start.

—Will Rogers

How does landlording pay off? You *make money* by buying properties, getting them ready, and managing them. You *create wealth* by finding and buying ones that fit your overall business strategy.

The Upside

Here's an example of how even a small annual profit adds up over time in the landlord business.

Twenty-five years ago, my neighbor's dad took a real estate seminar, read a book advertised on TV, and got into real estate buying. On the weekends he would buy properties, while keeping his full-time job. Instead of working only 40 hours a week, he began working 70 hours, which included overseeing his properties and serving his ten-

1

ants. Meanwhile, every day at the dinner table his wife would say, "Get rid of those properties! They are driving you crazy and stressing you out. I just don't know why you do it! Last month you made no money . . ."

Over a period of 20 years, this man bought houses, duplexes, and a small apartment building that had 80 units—all the while, he endured his wife's criticism. He has since passed away and his widow now lives in a $2 million beach house in Florida in the winter and in her other property up north in the summer. Her net worth is about $8 million, all because of what she called her husband's "headachy" rental property. Ironically, from his regular job, he received a pension worth only $400,000.

I have never seen an investment in which you can buy at 60 to 70 cents on the dollar, see your net worth go up, have a regular cash flow, and not have to use your own money. Every month—even the bad months, when you hate your landlord obligations—your tenants are still paying your mortgage while the value of your property goes up.

I have never seen a business in which people who have persistence, buy "smart," and are willing to work cannot succeed, regardless of their background. In this business, people with no money and little education can become millionaires. Imagine!

The Downside

Most landlords start by listening to an advisor who says, "You buy property and make hundreds of dollars a month in rent. You don't do anything." So I thought, "I won't have to do anything except check my bank account and watch the rent come in."

But like any other business in any part of the world, landlording has its rewards and it takes work. Minimizing the headaches and the stress that come with running this particular business will make the rewards even greater. This book tells you how to minimize those headaches.

Many landlords run their rental properties like a bad hobby—with neither a business plan nor policies and procedures (or, if they have them, they never follow them). Whether you own one property, five properties, or a hundred properties, you have a business with "customers" called tenants. To be successful, you need to know how to set up a business effectively and to establish standards for treating these customers.

Policies and Procedures

Most landlords, including myself at first, constantly feel stressed because Jean gets behind in her rent or Will disappears for months or Jim asks for leniency because his car broke down. Let's face it: When tenants call, it is not to tell you how much they appreciate your giving them a place to live. It is not to say they want to send you the rent early. They call with problems they want you to fix. When you check voice mail and listen to eight messages about their problems, your stress level goes up and your heart beats faster. You anticipate hassles; you fear you will spend too much time and money; you expect to hear excuses about paying the rent.

How do you handle these? By implementing your business policies and procedures. That way, you have no quick, on-the-spot decisions to make.

These policies and procedures cover basic property management duties and responsibilities, including the following, which are broken down into two categories—renting, and maintenance and repairs:

Renting

1. Screen prospective tenants on the phone, have them complete an application, and do not let anyone get a key before a lease is signed. Check with two of their previous landlords, verify that they are employed, and do a credit check and a criminal-background check.

2. Do not let a tenant move in until all repairs are completed and you get a signed Move-In Inspection Report from the tenant (see the form in Appendix B).
3. Get a deposit and rent in your hands in funds that are secured (e.g., a money order or a certified check).
4. Have tenants sign a repair cost sheet for any damage they may do. List the cost of various items, such as a clogged toilet or a lost key.
5. Have tenants sign a rent collection and eviction policy statement (which says, for example, that rent is due on the 1st of the month, is late on the 3rd, and that you evict on the 17th). Check with a lawyer to make sure the stated policies are legal. Treat every tenant the same; it's the law.
6. Have a retention program. For example, if tenants stay a year, they should receive a gift (assuming their rents have been paid on time).
7. Have a tenant referral program; pay them to refer other reliable tenants for your properties.
8. After your tenants move in, call to welcome them.

Maintenance and Repairs

1. Inspect all properties at least every 30 to 60 days.
2. List the kinds of repairs covered by the landlord and the kinds that are not.
3. Compose work orders for every repair, indicating the date, complaint, name, unit number, estimated completion date, cost estimate, actual date completed, and actual cost. Also include the name of the person who took the phone call and that of the person who did the repair.
4. Call to verify that repairs were done to provide quality control.
5. Guarantee that repairs will be made within three business days. If there are any delays, the landlord will refund the daily rent until the repair has been completed.
6. Get all repair bids in writing.
7. Charge all tenants for damages incurred.

8. Do not let tenants do repairs unless you have written agreements with them and you have screened them so that you know they can do them.
9. Do not let any repair people work for you unless you have checked two references and have conducted a credit check and a criminal-background check on them.
10. Get every bid for repair in detail, in writing, noting a stated finish date and a per-day penalty should the job not be completed on time.

 R O B E R T ' S   R U L E S

Have your policies and procedures in place, and stick to them. When you pay your note late at your bank, does some banker sit down in your living room and ask you about your problems, about who is sick in your family, and what a rough week you had? No! Lenders care about on-time payments—period. They enforce their policies and procedures to make sure their business thrives. Yes, you can bend the rules once in a while, but I can bet that every time you do, you will regret it.

Buying and Holding Real Estate

Consider this scenario: You are about to buy a house for $60,000 and it is appraised for $75,000. That's great. When you buy property, you want your net worth to go up. But if you bought that property for $75,000 and it is worth $75,000, you made a mistake. You are in the wrong business, reading the wrong book, and using the wrong information.

However, if you buy a property worth $75,000 and pay $60,000, your net worth goes up $15,000. Where else can you do that? Sure, you could buy a stock at $30 a share, then watch it go up to $45 and drop down to $26 a week later. The real estate business allows you to actually buy goods under market value—a rare business. The deals are out there. In fact, more deals probably exist within 45 minutes of where you live than you could ever imagine.

Let us say you have spotted a property you want to buy. Do you get a 15-year mortgage or a 30-year one? I suggest you make it at least a 20-year mortgage or higher, so you have the flexibility of paying it off earlier by putting additional dollars into your payment of principal. That way, if you get caught in a cash flow crunch, you're not obligated to pay the higher mortgage each month.

Property can appreciate significantly over the years or not at all. But even with a minor appreciation in your property's value over 20 years, your tenants have still paid rent every month and your equity still goes up while your debt goes down.

Vacancy/Repair Rate

Your goal is to bring in cash from rent paid by tenants, thus creating cash flow for your property business. But realize that you almost always have expensive repairs and unforeseen problems to deal with. So I will warn you now: Your property *will* create cash flow—*if* you buy right, *if* it is not overleveraged, and *if* you get good tenants. When you buy that property, the possibilities always look great. But in the real world, things happen.

Let's take the first duplex I bought, as an example. I had $400 a month in rent coming in from each tenant of the duplex. That comes to $9,600 a year in extra cash in my pocket—right? That is one of the beauties of a duplex—two tenants pay rent. So if one tenant vacates and I have to repaint, or repair windows, and the unit stays empty for a month or more, I still have money coming in. However, having a vacancy costs, so be careful—part of that $9,600 gain can fly out the door quickly.

In another example, if you have a property that rents for $900 a month and a mortgage of $700 a month, you make $200 a month—right? No, because you have to take into account the vacancy and repair factors. The government agency called HUD (Housing and Urban Development) builds in a 25 percent vacancy/repair rate when people apply for a mortgage. That means if the rent is $1,000 a month, HUD applies $250 of that to vacancy and repair expenses. From my experience, that's a low number!

With apartment complexes and multifamily projects, some property management companies calculate between 25 and 45 percent for vacancy, repair, and overhead costs. Others apply 40 to 50 percent—certainly more than 10 percent. My first business plan figured on a 10 percent vacancy and repair rate, which proved to be absurd.

Every market is different, so do your homework. In my experience, a rate of 20 to 40 percent would cover most single-family homes, condos, town houses, and duplexes, while 40 to 50 percent would cover apartment buildings. So remember to budget for the maintenance/repairs you intend to do and the possibility of time that passes without income.

 R O B E R T ' S   R U L E S

Make sure you build in a cushion when you set rent prices, and estimate a vacancy and repair rate that is realistic—more than 25 percent.

Of course, you can always hire others and, in fact, I advise most landlords to contract out as much work as is practical and affordable. Most people do not manage property well; it takes a special kind of crazy person to do it effectively and enjoy it. You are required to take on the role of directing the activities of those you hire, as a manager would, and to take care of administration details, as a human resources director would. Unless you contract it out as well, you are also the bookkeeping-and-collections department.

Realize that most businesses have about eight departments, and a full staff in each department who do all that's required to run a business. Your property business has eight departments, too, but a lot fewer people to run them.

CHAPTER 2

Types of Properties

When you choose not to decide—you still have made a choice!

–Neil Peart

What is the best type of property to own as a landlord? What is the worst? Every type of property has its advantages and disadvantages. The property pyramid in Figure 2.1 and the descriptions that follow will help you decide what types of properties might work best for you.

Single-Room Occupancies

Single-room occupancies (SROs) are low-cost properties such as older hotels, motels, and converted houses. With an SRO, people rent a bedroom by the week or by the night. (In fact, some people make money renting by "renting" a couch at $50 a week.)

Here's how it works. You can buy a house for $50,000 and rent it for $700 a month, for example. Or you can rent each of six rooms in the same house for $150 a week–that is, $900 a week, multiplied by four weeks, or a total of $3,600 a month.

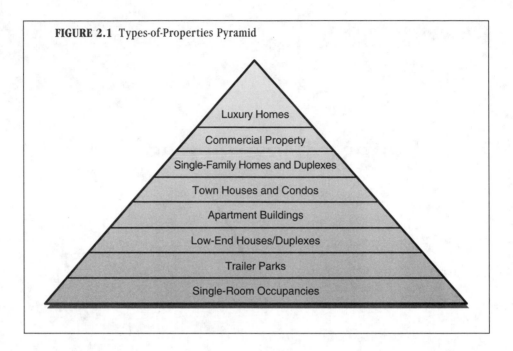

FIGURE 2.1 Types-of-Properties Pyramid

Luxury Homes

Commercial Property

Single-Family Homes and Duplexes

Town Houses and Condos

Apartment Buildings

Low-End Houses/Duplexes

Trailer Parks

Single-Room Occupancies

What are the disadvantages of SROs? You're constantly collecting rents, which can create hassles. You're likely to deal with crime and inevitable disagreements among people living in close quarters. And because they are usually located in low-income neighborhoods, SROs don't usually hold their value over time.

Trailer Parks

Trailer parks are next to the bottom in the pyramid. Their main advantage is that people who own low-end trailer parks can enjoy a high cash flow because they can rent units for $125 to $150 a week or for $500 to $600 a month. They pay about $1,500 to $3,000 for the trailers in the first place, but they can still get the same amount of rent as someone gets with a $50,000 house or a $60,000 duplex.

In terms of disadvantages, trailer parks require a lot of managing and maintenance. In any business, the more people you deal with, the more complicated everything becomes. And the more complicated it becomes, the greater the hassle. So if you have a trailer park property with 100 people living there, expect many more problems than if you have fewer houses and fewer renters.

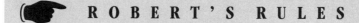

ROBERT'S RULES

Regardless of the type of house, the value of any dwelling depends on the neighborhood in which it is located. How do you get to know your targeted neighborhoods and the people in them? Walk the streets. Talk with people already living in the neighborhood and ask them how they like it. Note the kinds of cars people drive. Are they beat up and abandoned on the streets, or well maintained? Talk to members of the business community and the local chamber of commerce. Visit with other landlords and property managers. Are they making money? What problems do they handle every day? Most important, talk to police officers. Find out about crime rates in the area. Doing your homework will help you specifically define your market.

Another disadvantage is the time spent setting up leases and collecting rents. In addition to that, because people live in close quarters, you may have to deal in areas of conflict between neighbors. All this can lead to getting overwhelmed and burned out. You have to decide what your own pain level is in relation to profits earned.

Low-End Houses and Duplexes

You can certainly buy some houses and duplexes for next to nothing: $10,000 to $20,000. Indeed, in some parts of the United States, you can pay $8,000, even $6,000, or still less for a small house.

Again, they rent for about the same amount as a house or a duplex in medium-income areas that have more amenities: $300 or $400 a month, maybe $500 if rent is paid weekly. Other landlords are spending $40,000 to $60,000 on nicer homes and getting $550 a month. The quality of tenants may be different, but their cash flow is about the same and their return on investment is much higher.

ROBERT'S RULES

I strongly favor low-end duplexes and two-bedroom homes for highest profitability. They have lower initial costs and lower maintenance costs than upscale homes, and they're easier to rent in a down economy.

I always thought I was blessed in growing up in a middle-class family and neighborhood, but I have found that people in low-income neighborhoods are often friendlier and neater, more hardworking, and at times more honest, than people living in upscale neighborhoods.

When someone asks me how I deal with these tenants, I say, "Most of them care about their families and work real hard; they just might be having bad luck or not making as much money as other people. They're honest and hardworking." So put any preconceptions aside. Instead, do your research about neighborhoods in which you want to buy and decide with whom you want to work.

I strongly favor buying property in this category—for all the advantages stated here. It's where I've made my money. Duplexes equal cash flow. Instead of there being one tenant who pays rent, two tenants pay. Instead of collecting $450 to $500 a month for rent on a $50,000 property, you can likely get $900 or $1,000.

In some neighborhoods where it's usual for police to patrol frequently to keep the peace, consider the hassle factor. However, law-abiding people live in low-income houses, too!

It comes down to knowing your market. If you own a three-bedroom house in an upscale neighborhood and something breaks, your tenants want immediate service. Their new carpet had better be the best you can get. In the low- to moderate-income neighborhoods, people have often been treated badly by their previous landlords and don't expect any better treatment from you. You might have to spend the same amount of money to keep up with their expectations, or you might get by doing a little less. I've found that, in the low- to moderate-income neighborhoods, if the house is clean and in good repair, this often suffices. Again, know what people in your market expect.

Here's an example. In my low-income properties, I learned that people prefer having commercial-grade carpeting, the flat stuff without any fluff, over a higher grade of carpeting. Why? It's easier to clean without vacuum cleaners. They can sweep the commercial carpet with a broom. Once again, know your market, so you don't overspend or underspend on what you deliver.

Some people who go into the business of renting properties are used to having a marble kitchen and designer bushes out front. But if you put those features into a low-income property, the marble and those bushes disappear; in some neighborhoods, the tenants perceive no value in them.

Apartment Buildings

Next on the pyramid are apartment buildings. You can find them in low- to moderate-income areas or in upscale parts of town.

People often dislike living in apartments because they deal with more people, more traffic, and sometimes more disputes over things like parking spots. For these reasons, apartment investments come with high turnover rates—a definite disadvantage.

Another disadvantage is that an apartment building involves a lot of financial risk in one place. What if the city were to put the sewer plant next to your apartment building? Or what if the neighborhood were to develop a high crime rate? You've stashed a lot of eggs in one basket, and then you are faced with these problems.

Town Houses and Condos

Town houses and condos are considered a step up from apartment buildings. They require less maintenance than apartments, yet are more affordable than single-family homes. Many complexes also offer desirable amenities.

On the downside, monthly maintenance fees can hurt cash flow, and rules of the governing associations can curb tenants' freedom to make decisions. Town house living requires your tenants to adhere to the rules of living in a group, which can cause problems.

Single-Family Homes and Duplexes

Single-family homes and duplexes are a further step up on the pyramid. When it comes to three- to five-bedroom homes in decent areas of town, almost everybody wants one—complete with a big yard and all of the luxuries. According to national surveys, 97 percent of renters want to become homeowners of a single-family home in a good neighborhood.

But also, 99 percent want to live in a place that's more expensive than they can realistically afford. The low-income family wants a three-bedroom house in a neighborhood that's safer than the one they came from. The middle-class family wants to live in the five-bedroom home in a more upscale neighborhood. Others want to live in a ten-room mansion and have horses and a beach and all of the other luxuries. The point is this: It's human nature to buy or rent a home that's a step higher than one can afford. That's why it's important to screen and prequalify any prospective tenants carefully (see Chapter 5).

An advantage is that you can have single-family homes in different neighborhoods in the community and even around the country, thus spreading your financial risk. That means that if properties in one neighborhood appreciate, while those in another depreciate, you can maintain some overall stability. True, you will spend more time driving around taking care of these properties than you will with an apartment building in a single location, but it comes down to the best return on your time and money.

A disadvantage is that single-family homes have a lower cash flow than other properties. You have to spend much more money to purchase one house. Because you deal with only one tenant (or one couple) with a single-family home, he or she will probably stay a long time, so you'll have less turnover than you will with renting a duplex or an apartment building.

Also, regarding big houses and high-end homes with three, four, and five bedrooms, when someone moves out, your costs are greater than they are for the options lower on the pyramid. Thirty days without receiving rent requires a lot of money to cover a larger mortgage. You also have more carpets, more walls, and a lot more paint to cover them, so having a home is clearly a bigger expense. If your tenant moves out of your five-bedroom home, fixing it could cost $5,000 to $10,000. Few landlords anticipate this high expense; they optimistically think that people will move in, stay for several years, and only incur a cost of $20 a year to fix a leaky sink. Then, when they move out, you have to do a makeover. And that costs money.

Commercial Property

Smart landlords make a lot of money with commercial property. Commercial tenants tend to be a lot different from residential ones. For one thing, they won't call you up and scream that the sink leaks. Generally, the commercial lease requires them to take responsibility for property maintenance; you just rent them the building. The tenants fix it up themselves, take care of it, add to it to meet their needs, etc.

However, commercial property is much harder to finance than residential real estate. Almost any lender will give you some kind of loan on a house, but commercial property is more risky because it is tied more closely to the economy. And when the economy goes down, property could sit empty—even for a year or two.

Realize that if your tenant moves out, you could spend thousands of dollars finding the next commercial tenant (and you could lose money due to vacancy time). When negotiating a lease, you could spend hundreds of thousands of dollars on a buildout to suit a tenant. So although some people can find good deals on commercial property, they need to be more cautious because their success will be tied to economic trends in the community.

Luxury Houses

Luxury housing, at the top part of the pyramid, can be the most lucrative option, but it's also the riskiest. When I met with my banker, he said, "Robert, we have done a study of Nashville. We think the rental market there is going into the tank. We are really concerned about the low-income area where you have bought houses."

I stopped him right there: "Wait a minute. You did a study on these 2,000-unit luxury apartment buildings they just put up in the high-end part of town. Yes, if the economy goes down and things turn, buildings may well have a high vacancy rate. But when people move out of there, where do they go? They come over to my duplexes, my bread-and-butter houses."

Other Options

As the population gets older, studies show, the fastest-growing areas of the country are in resort areas and smaller towns. Because people like a small-town lifestyle, these locations are really going to grow, according to futuristic-trend magazines.

It might therefore behoove a landlord to look at locations in resort and beach communities. You could potentially make a lot of money by buying property in these areas. You would most likely need to hire an on-site manager for your property there.

Some people reason that they can buy a place at the beach (or in the mountains, or wherever), and that rent pays for all the property expenses. You can do that, but be careful. Resort properties are extremely vulnerable to marketplace ups and downs, and lose their popularity and value quickly.

Best Recommendation: Low-End Houses and Duplexes

This is why I love "bread-and-butter," low- to moderate-income housing: You can always rent these units, even if you do not get as much rent as you want or they stay empty longer. Also, you can always sell them, even in bad economic times. Studies of housing have shown that, even during the real estate recession of the late 1980s, low- to moderate-income housing still sold well.

People have to live somewhere. So during poor economic times, here's what happens to low-income housing:

- You may not get as big a security deposit, and you may have longer vacancies.
- You may also have to give incentives to low-income people or treat them better than ever.
- You may have to spend time collecting rent from those who pay slowly.

Even when you take all these factors into account, you can, generally speaking, continue to do well with low-income-property investments. On the other hand, those who speculated on the luxury apartments and the big commercial buildings in the late 1980s got hurt badly.

R O B E R T ' S   R U L E S

- In my opinion, basic low-end housing is where solid gains can be made

- Every type of property has its advantages and disadvantages for landlords.

- The properties that have more people usually generate greater cash flow, but also require more involvement from the landlord.

- Location, density, the type of property you buy, and—most important—the type of people you will be managing will determine your workload and management demands. Consider all of these before buying properties and/or managing them.

CHAPTER 3

Getting Started as a Landlord

Success follows doing what you want to do. There is no other way to be successful.

—Malcolm Forbes

You found a good deal on a house, so you bought it and you're a landlord for the first time. Next, you get your place ready for your first "customers," your tenants. And after they move in, you hope you never hear from them again. Your goal is to have tenants pay rent and never have a reason to call, except to wish you a merry Christmas.

Ready to Rent

"Ready to rent" is a relative term; some people believe that if the property has a door and a roof that doesn't leak much, it's ready to rent. For me, "ready to rent" means the place has to be clean, appealing, and in good condition—when customers walk in the door, it should look better than other places they have seen. As a result of this readiness, you attract the type of tenant who will care for it.

There is nothing wrong with doing the minimum to get your place ready to rent; you just have to know the renters in your market and what meets their minimum expectations. But a clean, attractive home in a good neighborhood will always rent faster, and for a higher price, than an unattractive one in an undesirable area.

Attracting Your First Tenants

When your new property is ready to rent, it's time to advertise. Learn from the local real estate agents and use signage. (The National Association of REALTORS® says about 88 percent of all homes are sold to people who drive by a home and see a For Sale sign. That means the minute your place is empty or even before that, put up a For Rent sign.) Even if you're worried about the idea that it may signal vandals to come and damage the unit, you can still put up a sign. If the neighborhood is prone to vandalism, your sign won't make a difference. And if so, maybe you don't want to have a property there, anyway.

Target Your Market

You want to target your advertising toward the kinds of renters you prefer to have on your property, without breaking Fair Housing laws. In my experience, the best renters are people who are older and who, generally speaking, are likely to stay in one place and live quietly. They tend to behave much differently than young people in their 20s who are focused on socializing, can be slobs, and commonly move every four months. So you may be wise to target your market to older people.

Remember that housing laws don't allow you to discriminate on the basis of a person's race, creed, color, religion, or disability. Through your advertising strategy, you can target specific age groups, or workers in a particular line of work (e.g., teachers, police officers, graduate students, or employees from a particular company in the area).

The Advertising Supersystem

If you run an ad in the local newspaper to rent a property in a hot market, your phone will ring off the wall. Then you'd answer every call by saying, "Yes, it is a two-bedroom with one bath. You take Gallatin Road and take a left on Neill, and it is down a block and a half . . . . Yes, on that street . . . . Yes, it has a refrigerator and a stove. Would you like to come and see it? Okay . . . ." All this information could have been—and should have been—in your ad in the first place.

You have just spent four hours repeating the same things. During three of those hours, you talked to people who are looking for a house or an apartment in another part of town. Most callers aren't even interested in what you have to offer, so it becomes a complete waste of their time—and of yours.

Put as much information as possible into your ad: "3-bedroom, 2-bath . . . East Nashville . . . take Gallatin Road, go left on Neill . . . 110 Neill Street . . . rent $450." Then include the information in a separate voice-mail message, which costs only $15 a month. Give out *that* phone number in the ad. When people call, they hear the following: "Congratulations! You have made an excellent choice in calling the home hotline today. We have some wonderful places for you to choose from. Now, here is what you do: Grab a piece of paper and a pencil, because I am about to give you some important information. We have a two-bedroom, one-bath, in a nice location near schools and shopping. Go to Gallatin Road and take a left on Neill. It is a block and a half down on the left, at 110 Neill."

Then you can talk about any of its features: a remodeled kitchen, a spacious living room, central air-conditioning and heating, appliances, ceiling fans—whatever. Put in some marketing pizzazz. If you don't want to record the message yourself, find someone with a good telephone voice that will get people excited. Remember to speak slowly and distinctly in the message; it is your company's first contact with potential tenants and you want the right person to come and see the place.

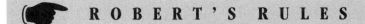

ROBERT'S RULES

Use a voice-mail message that includes all of the information you want tenants to know. Speak clearly and slowly. Repeat all phone numbers and addresses twice. Also, find someone with an easily understood, interesting voice. For example, I often hire a woman who has a British accent; she records my voice-mail messages.

Creating Your Voice-Mail Message

To cover the details, write down all the questions renters will ask: "Where is the nearest school?" "How do you get there?" "What main streets are near there?" "Is there a bus line nearby?" Then put the answers on the voice-mail message. Give directions and say, "If you are interested, drive by and take a look. Then give us a call [at another number] and arrange an appointment."

If you have more than one place to rent, you can add another mailbox to your voice-mail message for a few more dollars. Your message would say: "Press 1 for North Macon; press 2 for South Macon; press 3 for luxury apartments." If you have still more places, put them all on the voice-mail message. This way, you can sort out the renters you don't want and help screen the ones you want to deal with.

Consider this message: "Hey, this is a great place! We really look forward to having you move in, and we hope we can work something out. However, you should know we are going to do a credit and background check and a criminal-background check."

When I used to give that information over the phone, some people would just hang up. By using voice mail, you can sort out potentially risky tenants (although this system doesn't always work) but you can eliminate some riffraff, just by using your voice mail. A word of caution: If the market is slow in your community and nobody is calling about rentals, pick up the phone quickly and immediately, 24 hours a day.

Use these tips:

- Make your message exciting and enticing.
- For each place, give the location, any special features, and the rent range.
- Also, tell callers they will be screened. If you have concerns about scaring away a good tenant, add something like, "We don't expect perfect credit or perfect people. But we will do a credit check and factor that into the decision." This will sort out those people whose furniture landed on the sidewalk after their last eviction.
- Don't give your home telephone number to tenants or prospective tenants. Instead, use the voice mail. It's great because it doesn't even ring, because no phone is attached. Also, discount voice mail is available nationwide for about $15 a month; you can get 20 boxes, with 50 messages. Check with your local landlord association for resources of this kind.
- Quick customer service is a must, so check your voice mail regularly and return all phone calls promptly. I recommend that you check messages every two hours during the business day and that you return all calls within four hours.

This supersystem really works. We also use it to sell homes. Instead of your picking up the phone and answering 4,000 questions, the voice-mail message tells people to call the hotline. If they are seriously interested, they will listen to the message for the full three or four minutes. This way, we weed out a lot of people and save a lot of time.

Setting the Rent

The first question potential renters ask is "How much is the rent?" Our voice-mail message doesn't tell people our rent amounts. We might give them a range—say, $350 to $450—but not a specific figure.

So when I call them back, I ask, "How much are you looking to spend?"

This one sentence could make you $10,000 over the next five or ten years. I learned this from Jeffrey Taylor, author of the *Mr. Landlord* newsletter, which you can find at <www.MrLandlord.com>. When I started out, I would say the rent was $425 and that's what I got. Sometimes a person talked me down to $410 or even $395. But then, when I would ask, "How much are you looking to spend?" the person might reply, "I want to pay $200 a month." Then I know instantly that the person is not the right customer for this unit. But she also might also say, "I am looking for something in the $485 range." That just gave me a $60 rent increase. So this is my lucky day. I may even be generous and say the rent is only $475.

So don't just settle for an arbitrary rent figure; let the market set it. You will be amazed by what can happen. (However, avoid getting into a verbal match on the phone: "Well, how much are you charging?" "Well, how much do you want to pay?" "How much are you charging?", and so forth.)

Let's do the math: If I were going to get $425 a month and, instead, got $475, that would be $50 a month extra. Multiply that by 12 and it becomes $600 a year. If I own 100 units and do that with all of the units, it adds up to $60,000. And to earn that extra 60 grand, I ask a simple question, consistently, of every prospective tenant. That one question has made me an extra $30,000 to $40,000 in just two years. Keep doing that and it adds up to a lot of money.

Never let tenants give you a partial first payment. You have probably heard the excuses: "Well, I am getting paid on Friday. I have $400 now and I will get another $200 next week; then in two weeks my mother will give me another $100, and. . . . " If they cannot afford to pay rent plus deposit money up front, they won't be able to afford to pay rent for the following months. Make the collecting of full rent a standard practice.

Higher Rates Attract Better Tenants

Suppose I rent each place I own in one neighborhood for $495, while other landlords in the area rent similar properties for $425. You might say I am charging more than the market rate. Yet I guarantee that the person who pays $495 for rent will be a better tenant than the one who pays $425. If prospective tenants hem and haw about the extra $70 dollars, they likely can't pay their rent consistently, even at the lower rate.

So don't shy away from charging a somewhat higher rent to attract tenants. I guarantee that the more money people are willing to pay for rent, the better tenants they will be.

Special Rent Programs

Especially if you have several places to rent over time, you might offer special programs. Let us say, the basic rent is $425; the deluxe package, with appliances and the miniblinds, is a little extra but worth the cost. The deluxe package is an extra $30 a month. Remember that this is your business. Get paid for everything.

When you go to a car showroom, not all of the cars are priced the same. The salesperson says, "If you want the undercoating, that's an extra $800. And you want the four-speaker stereo? That's an extra $20 a month on your lease." Similarly, you should spell out what you are providing: appliances, television, higher-grade carpeting, ceiling fans, a brass kickplate, and carpet cleaning done every six months. Whatever an item costs you, double the cost and charge that amount. In this business, make everything you do the basis for a profit center.

Regarding pest control, tell your tenants this: "The place is $425 unless you want pest control (which we do anyway and it costs us $6 a unit a month). For you, it is an extra $19.95 a month. I highly recommend it." People will go for it because they have already signed up for the $425 to $500 range. (Again, anything you provide should be positioned as an add-on.) Explain to tenants: "We normally spray once or twice a year, but with the deluxe service, we spray every month. That's an extra $19.95."

A word of caution: In most states, the law requires you to keep your properties free from bugs and rodents, and you therefore need to spray more often. However, the tenants' own habits often create most of the pest problems. If they keep the units clean and relatively sanitary, it is likely that infestation won't happen. If they do not keep them clean, they'll almost certainly get bugs.

Application Fees

Our policy is to make application fees nonrefundable. If you are spending time—whether it is 3 minutes or 30 minutes—helping them fill out an application, it's your time, and time is money; you are running a business. Remember to comply with Fair Housing laws; if you charge one person an application fee, you must charge everyone.

R O B E R T ' S   R U L E S

Make every operation in your business a profit center. Even the application process can be a profit center. For example, if it costs $20 to run credit and background checks, ask the prospective tenant to pay $25 or $30 for these.

Pay attention to your market, of course. If other property managers do free credit checks because the market is tight, you need to absorb that cost, too. But if they charge $25, match that amount or go higher. Most landlords for single-family houses don't charge an application fee but landlords for the big apartment complexes certainly do. Take a hint from them.

When I told people who work for me that we charge application fees, and that I would split the profit with them, they started thinking, "I want to make some money. I am going to try harder to take in more applications." It thus became a good motivator.

CHAPTER 4

Handling Maintenance Requests

I don't know the key to success, but the key to failure is trying to please everybody.

–Bill Cosby

The biggest complaint most renters have is that the landlord won't fix anything. Along with that, a renter says, "I've been calling my landlord every day for ten days and I never get a call back."

When I interviewed 200 tenants before I started in this business, people told me stories about toilets that were not working for 45 days and about the landlord who ignored their daily phone calls. So their response was, "Well, if the landlord doesn't care, why should I? I am going to rip out the toilet and throw it through a window!" After waiting 45 days, I might do the same. That's why we created the following policies.

Repair Policies

Policy #1: We Require Written Requests for Repairs

If you ever go to court because tenants have sued you for evicting them (if you have lots of tenants, that is likely to happen), tenants will argue that you never fixed anything. You and your attorney can respond by saying, "Where is the written request? It is required by the terms of the lease."

In practice, we allow tenants to make repair requests over the phone. After all, we use our voice mail as a repair hotline and our message says: "Superior Properties's maintenance line. This line is checked twice a day. If you have a problem, someone will get back to you and we will get it fixed in a timely fashion. Please remember, we cannot make a repair if you don't leave your name, address, phone number, and a description of the problem. If you don't do these things, we cannot fix it. Remember, leave your name, address, etc." You have to ask for the name and number twice; if you only say it once, tenants won't comply.

Twice a day, someone in our office checks the repair/maintenance line and writes down every request received. Typically, we receive about 15 calls—half of them from the same person calling every 15 minutes. We return every call (remember that our policy is to return all calls within 24 hours) and we deal with the situation as soon as possible.

Without a voice-mail system, here's what a tenant usually says: "Hey, Mr. Robert! My sink don't work, and it's really maddening. I can't believe it's been leaking for two days now. I need you to fix it right now!"

When I used to field these calls, I'd be polite on the phone, but inside I'd be seething. Sometimes in my frustration, I would argue back, even get defensive. Then I'd drop everything and arrange to send a repairperson over. Now the tenants can yell at the voice-mail system instead. All I need is their address, their phone number, and the nature of the problem. With this system, we eliminate a lot of frustration and save hundreds of hours of direct fielding of calls.

Policy #2: We Return All Phone Calls within 24 Hours on a Business Day

This policy isn't always easy to follow because some of our tenants don't have telephones (or their phones have been disconnected).

In these cases, we mail them a letter and they therefore receive a response the next day.

This 24-hour return-call policy makes good sense, whatever business you are in. In real estate, if you actually call back within a day, you are in the top 5 percent of those who do. You don't need to do anything else; you just call tenants back, and do it with empathy. They are usually upset, worried, and under stress when they call. Just acknowledging that fact lowers stress levels significantly. Your acknowledgment of their situation won't fix the problem but, instead of being agitated and upset with you, they will feel much better.

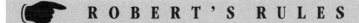

ROBERT'S RULES

Return all phone calls within one business day. It is good business, people appreciate the attention, and it clearly sets you apart from other landlords. And, combined with the three-day repair guarantee, it shows you care.

Policy #3: We Guarantee to Do Repairs within Three Days

That means if a tenant calls us and requests a repair (e.g., the sink leaks, the doorknob falls off, the plumbing stops working), we guarantee to fix it within three business days. (Of course, the problem must be legitimate—if a tenant breaks a window, then demands we fix it, that's not legitimate.)

To back up our guarantee, if we do not fix the problem within three business days, the tenants get their daily rent back, in cash, until we do fix it. For example, if it takes five days to make the repair, instead of three, we give back two days' rent. (Our policy excludes special situations such as waiting to get parts.)

Renters love my repair policy. It communicates the fact that we are serious about keeping their place nice. It also says, "We don't want you to move out; we want to take good care of you!" I suggest setting up a three-day repair guarantee and making a big deal about it when a prospective tenant first looks at your property. Put this repair policy in writing, in large print, so it is clear. If your maintenance people don't respond within three days, be proactive. Call your tenant as soon as you know about the delay and send the money promised. This builds a lot of loyalty. That happened with Katie, who had to wait six days for a repair to be completed. It cost me $30 to make the situation right. But since then, she has told all of her friends about the landlord who actually sent her $30 when he didn't have to. This built thousands of dollars worth of goodwill. Good service is good marketing.

In rental situations, the landlord takes responsibility for repairs. This is mandatory. (In lease-option situations, landlords don't do repairs—see Chapter 9 for more details; also, refer to the discussion of no-fault maintenance, in Chapter 6.) We have a clause in our lease that asks that repair requests be put in writing.

Policy #4: We Call the Tenant a Day or Two after the Repairs to Follow Up

Whenever a repair gets completed, the person who did it leaves a note on the tenant's door, with a message that, in effect, says, "We came here right away and we are on top of it. Thanks for letting us know about it." We also do something others rarely do: After repairs are completed, we make a follow-up phone call. What often happens—even with the perfect repairperson (and I haven't found that person yet, although I have been looking for ten years)—is that the problem wasn't fixed correctly or another problem has shown up. It takes just a few minutes to say, "Katie, this is Robert of Superior Properties, just checking to make sure your repair was done properly and everything is okay." If she is not there, we leave the message on her voice mail. The quality control procedure that takes only seconds clearly sets us apart from other landlords. It goes back to our basic premise of treating tenants properly—they stay if you do, they tell their friends, and they take care of the property.

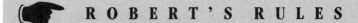

ROBERT'S RULES

Quality control is so important—and so rare—in property management. After every repair call, contact the tenant by phone or by letter, ask if the repair was done properly, and make sure the tenant is satisfied with the work. This also helps you find out whether your repairpeople are doing their jobs properly.

When tenants request repair work and your repairperson is available today, but you can't get in touch with the tenants, can you go in? Property laws governing this kind of entry differ from state to state, but here's my belief: If your tenants have requested a repair, they have asked you to come in. We call and leave word that our repairperson is coming by.

Remember that when tenants rent an apartment, it becomes *their* place, not yours—even though you own it. Because it's their home, you need to let them know when you are coming. To cover yourself legally, make a phone call and send something in writing. Always let them know first. If you go in unannounced, you are trespassing and you risk getting sued. Check with a qualified attorney in your area for a clarification of the laws in your state. If tenants sue you, they will probably win.

Six Steps for Handling Repair Requests

1. Set up a maintenance system that includes voice mail or an answering machine.
2. Check messages twice a day and write down all requests.
3. Return all calls within 24 hours.
4. Schedule repairs within three business days.

5. Let tenants know, via phone or in writing, when the repair-person will come over.
6. Follow every completed repair with a phone call to tenants and ask if they are satisfied.

Policies for Dealing with Contractors

Many landlords do their own maintenance and repairs. As for me, I can't fix anything, even if it's changing a lightbulb. In real estate, your best money is made by finding deals and buying properties, not in doing maintenance work. However, many landlords save a lot of money by keeping their places in good repair through their own work. The truth is, no one will do it better than you because nobody else has the vested interest you have in the property.

It's important to understand that your time is money. Determine how much you can pay someone to paint the place or to fix the carpet or sink. I am not saying you should stop doing maintenance or change the whole way you run your business. I am saying that it is a business! And just like the president of IBM can probably fix a computer, he doesn't use his time to run over to somebody's office and make sure the computer there works right. He spends his time managing his business, making deals, etc.

In real estate, you could spend three days putting a deal together and making $12,000. Or you could spend those three days painting an apartment and cleaning the carpets, whereas you could have paid someone $12 or $15 an hour to do all of that. Ask yourself: "What business am I in? What makes me the most money? And how do I want to spend my time?"

Think of it this way: You could probably change the oil in your car. But you could risk destroying the car's engine. Or you could pay $19.95 to someone who does it every day and you would know it would be done right. It's the same principle.

Policy #1: We Get Every Repair Bid in Writing

Then we break it down into two elements: cost of materials and labor and the time the repair will take.

Each bid should include:

- The date the repair is ordered
- The expected date of completion
- The name of the person who will do the work
- The items that will be repaired—down to the doorstop
- Provisions for a per-day penalty if the work is not completed on schedule

To show why we follow this policy carefully, here's a typical conversation between a landlord and a contractor—and one you want to avoid:

"What will replacing this window cost?" "Well, you know, the glass for the window is $35!" "And how long will it take you?" "Well, you know, I have to drive over here and pick it up, and then put it in—probably about two hours." "How much are you bidding me?" "Well, $195!" "So with $35 for the materials, that would be $160 for the two hours of labor—that's $80 an hour. In that case, teach me how to fix windows!"

Is that a fair price for a window replacement? Here's another example: "How much will you charge to paint this place?" "Well, it is about $600 to paint this house." "How much is the paint?" "Well, I need ten gallons; let's say $100." "How long will it take you?" "With me and another guy; all day." "So two guys, working one day, are going to make 500 bucks. That's $250 per person per day—an eight-hour day, at $25 an hour."

Is that fair? You decide. These examples show why you should break down every repair bid into materials and labor, and get an estimate on the time it will take. I know roofers who make $500 an hour and painters who make $200 an hour. But they aren't going to make that much off of me! They deserve to get paid but don't let them go overboard. Break down every bid and make sure you don't get ripped off.

Policy #2: We Always Do a Credit and a Criminal-Background Check before Hiring a Contractor

Get to know the people you hire, especially if they are going into your tenants' homes. First, do a credit check and a criminal-background check, just as you would do with a tenant. Let me strongly emphasize this: Do not let any maintenance person or contractor into any of your properties without first doing a background check. If you hire known thieves or rapists and they rob or harm one of your tenants, you may be held responsible. You should have known that information before hiring them.

Policy #3: We Make Sure Everyone Who Works More Than 25 Hours a Week for Us has Workers' Compensation Insurance

If workers get hurt on the job and they don't have workers' comp, they look to the employer for medical coverage. However, if the workmen do only one job every three weeks or so for you and also work for other people, you are probably safe in not requiring a workers' comp policy (see Chapter 12). Either way, you want all evidence of insurance in writing.

Policy #4: We Never Pay until the Job Is Completed

I sometimes pay contractors 30 percent to 40 percent up front, but I want to know that a sink is fixed before I pay the rest of the money owed. I have the tenant call me, or I look for myself, to make sure the repair was completed. Some contractors call to say, "I have finished and I want to get paid now. Meet me today over at . . ." (and they name a restaurant or a bar). Remember that *you* are running the business. Do not let contractors run you.

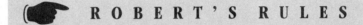

ROBERT'S RULES

If you use your own employees to do repairs, track their time on each repair call. Make sure they are really putting in a full day. Track their work orders and the estimated time for doing a job versus the actual time. Let them know about your tracking procedures—it will help motivate them to do good work.

When working with contractors:

- Explain your policies up front. Give contractors a typewritten copy of your policies and procedures.
- Insist on seeing an invoice before you pay them.
- Verify with the tenant that the job was done well before you pay a contractor.
- Pay according to your regular payment schedule.

CHAPTER 5

Finding Good Tenants

Look twice before you leap.

–Charlotte Brontë

Two-thirds of all landlords, when they screen their tenants, simply look at them and think, "She looks nice, and she was really polite—I will rent her a place." Or, "This guy has a wad of cash in his pocket—he gets the key." Most landlords in fact do not properly screen their applicants, yet screening is the most important part of the process. Let me share a story to illustrate this point.

Breaking My Own Rules

During my first few years in business, I didn't have my policies and procedures in place, although I've now followed them diligently for several years. But only a short time ago, Robert—Mr. Seminar Guy, Mr. Landlord, Mr. Expert—broke every rule he had ever set.

For example: I had a property at 1224 Lillian Street, a pretty house in a decent area of East Nashville. An elderly, sweet-sounding woman called to rent it—I'll call her Grandma Smith. She needed a place to live, so I met with her. She said she wanted to live by herself in this two-bedroom house. She promised to bake me a treat and give me a gift, and she was thanking God she had met me. So I fell in love with this sweet, grandmotherly lady. She urged me to decide about her right away because her other place was being sold and she needed to move. I immediately got out a lease. We signed it and she gave me some money up front—it is always exciting when someone waves money in front of you. I even helped her move in.

I owned seven houses on Lillian Street. So Grandma Smith moved in, and within 36 hours I fielded eight calls an hour from her neighbors, who said, "Robert, what have you done? You usually run a good ship. But what is going on over at that house you just rented?" A guy had been hanging out in the backyard wielding a knife; someone had beaten up someone else; the police were hovering. I went over to the house and—I am not exaggerating—saw 20 to 25 people living there. Some people were even sleeping in the toolshed in the backyard—it was their home. Grandma Smith's extended family looked like they had stepped out of the movie *Deliverance* and had moved in with her. Meanwhile, Grandma Smith was drunk and had passed out on the couch; I couldn't even communicate with her.

I knew I should have evicted them then and there, but they told me Grandma Smith was sick, and that she would get rid of all these people. They promised this would not go on: it was an accident, somebody else's fault.

So I waited another week or so. In the meantime, the police kept going over there, the neighbors kept calling, and other tenants got ready to move out of the neighborhood. I hesitated way too long. So I filed for eviction and showed up in court for the case: *Shemin Superior Properties* v. *Grandma Smith*. Grandma Smith wasn't there. I think, "Great, I have a default judgment." But when the judge called the names on the roster, an attractive young woman stood up. Here's how the dialogue went:

> "My name's Veronica, and I'm here."
> "Who are you?" asked the judge.
> "Well, Granny couldn't make it, so I'm here in her place."

The judge then asked me, "What's going on here?"

"Your Honor," I started, "We have criminal activity. One person is named on the lease and 24 people are living in this house. They are taking drugs in the house; it is a drug den."

Suddenly, Veronica jumped up and said, "Now, wait a minute, your Honor. I gotta talk here."

"Well," replied the judge. "What do you have to say for yourself?"

"Now that is not true!" she said. "That man over there is lying . . . . We do not do drugs in the house. She will not let us take drugs in the house. She makes us go out in the front yard."

This case turned into a three-day drug eviction, Grandma Smith's "family" finally got out, and I learned two valuable lessons: (1) I should never overrule my own policies and procedures; and (2) when a problem erupts, I must deal with it immediately—evict and move on.

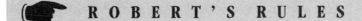

R O B E R T ' S   R U L E S

Every time I have deviated from my policies and procedures, I have regretted it. When something goes wrong, don't hesitate—take action immediately and stick to your own rules.

Screening Questions

Having learned my lesson, I now screen tenants on the phone as thoroughly as possible. Most new landlords go out and meet prospective tenants, talk to them, get them to fill out applications, go back to the office, do a check and find out they have never paid a bill on time and are therefore wanted in several states. They have just wasted at least two hours of valuable time.

Instead, spend three minutes on the phone and ask these questions:

- Where are you living now?
- How long have you lived there?
- Why are you moving?

The question "Why are you moving?" screens out many tenants. If they are currently living with family members, watch out. They may have been evicted from a rental for not paying the rent, and now even their mother is kicking them out because they cause trouble. Consider any prospective tenants currently living with family a big risk.

Here's a typical conversation:

"Where are you living now?"
"I live on 100 Apple Street."
"How long have you been there?"
"Six months."
"Why are you moving?"

The answers vary and can be very humorous:

"Well, my landlord won't fix anything."
"See, I got into a fistfight with my landlord last week."
"Well, I ain't paid the rent in three months, and the landlord says I gotta move."
"Gee, I just got evicted yesterday. My stuff's out on the corner—I need a place to live."

Of course, we run into hard-core liars and storytellers, but most people tell the truth on the phone. And if they don't, we will catch them in a lie before they'd receive a key from us.

Another example:

"Where are you living now? How long have you been there?"

"I was there for four years. I want to move because I want to switch neighborhoods."

"Why didn't you like that neighborhood? Why? Why? Why?"

Don't come across as though you are interrogating a witness in a court case. If you are friendly and polite, most people will answer truthfully.

If a prospective tenant says he lived in one place for four years, ask, "How long did you live at your previous residence?" "Oh, I lived near there for six years." That's a good response. On the other hand, if he says, "Well, I lived here for six months; and before that, I was in this other place for three months; and before that, it was two months over there . . . that was right after I got out of jail"—obviously, he's trouble.

Next question: "Where do you work?" If the person says, "I don't work," or, "I haven't worked in a year," keep probing, because landlords cannot discriminate against people who live on disability insurance. In my experience, a lot of people who don't work prove to be great tenants. They are on some kind of disability insurance or another government program. Nothing wrong with that—just be sure to know their exact situation.

Another question: "How do you pay your rent?" "Well, I get a $4,000 disability check every month" or "I don't work; the trust fund will pay it; call my attorney." These answers are okay. Here are some dubious ones: "Where do you work?" "Over there at a machine shop." "How long have you been there?" "Three months." That's not a good response. "Where were you before that?" "I worked over at the other machine shop." "How long were you there?" "Two months." That's not good. "Where were you before that?" The reply: "I lasted about three weeks before I got arrested, and had a fight with the owner." Here's another conversation: "Where do you work?" "Over here." "How long have you been there?" "Three and a half years." This is clearly a better response.

Ask these key questions on the phone, before you waste time meeting someone who is wrong for a particular situation.

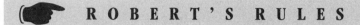

ROBERT'S RULES

I have learned to protect my time and to screen callers quickly. That way, any prospective renter who could cause trouble doesn't get very far. It's better to have a vacancy for a while than to rent to a possibly difficult tenant.

Credit Check

Next in the screening conversation, I say, "We do a credit check on everybody who moves into our place." Now, if you are a landlord for low-end rentals at, say, $100 a month, you think you might not need to do a credit check; you know it won't be a good one. But I still do a credit check because I want to know the person with whom I am dealing. So I say, "We really want to work with you. Mostly, we grade on honesty. I don't expect you to have perfect credit to rent my little place, but we will still do a credit check. Before I do, please tell me what kind of credit I am going to find."

One of two things will happen: Either they will be truthful or they will lie. If they lie and say, "Oh, my credit is great!," then we pull the report and it is 19 pages long, they are out because they lied. But if they say, "My credit is not perfect. I have some problems" say, "We work with people like you all the time. We don't expect perfection." Then if they say, "I got behind on my bills a year and a half ago, and had a lot of medical bills, but I have always paid my rent on time," the chances are greater that you would rent a low-income property to someone like that anyway. We want them to tell us their circumstances first. Then if they pass all the other tests, we fill out the application while on the phone.

Criminal-Background Check

Next, I say, "We are going to do a criminal-background check." At that point, some people just hang up the phone. If they stay on, I ask, "Do you mind if we do that?" People tell us incredible things: "A couple of years ago, I got in a fight at a bar and had an assault charge." I usually say, "Well, that happens." When I ask these questions over the phone, most people tell the truth, but you have to probe.

After a lot of practice screening people over the phone, I can determine, with 90 percent accuracy, if that person will work out. So can you. You may make a mistake or get fooled by a pro like Grandma Smith, but if you screen them well, you can have a near-perfect success rate.

As you consider the facts, common sense will rule. You think, "This guy has been on the job five years, he lived in the previous place six years, and he says his credit is good. He'll probably get in if what he says checks out." But if a guy says, "I never lived for more than four months anywhere in my life, and now I live with my family and I don't have a job" common sense tells you he is out.

Authorizations

To do a credit check or a criminal-background check, the law requires you to have a signed release that gives you permission to do the check. You may not do a formal check on a prospective tenant, or on an employee or a contractor, without his or her signature.

If prospective tenants pass your verbal screening, you can meet them, fill out an application, and get written permission to do credit and background checks. Many screening services do all of this for you. Ask for references from your local landlord association, apartment managers' association, or similar groups. This service calls employers, verifies previous landlords, and does credit and criminal-background checks. One national company is Tenant Check; Background America is another. Many of these agencies are run by former police officers and detectives. They charge $15 to $30 for each check—a cost the tenant pays for. Our company subscribes to the local Credit Bureau for about $20 a month. Then it costs ten cents to pull each credit report. If you are doing any volume at all, it makes sense to do that, too.

In some states, a law called Megan's Law requires a landlord to check out prospective tenants and make sure they are not child-molesters. Check locally with your attorney for details about complying with that law.

 R O B E R T ' S   R U L E S

What is your time best spent on—finding good deals and investing, chasing down paperwork and doing background checks, or doing maintenance and repairs? Figure out what business you want to be in and farm out the rest. If you see yourself as a real estate investor and landlord, as I see myself, I recommend you hire a company to do your background checks, credit checks, and criminal-record research.

Verifying Income

In the screening interview, a prospective tenant might tell you he makes $9,000 a month. So ask him, "How are you making it?" If he answers, "I cannot tell you!", you might suspect he is dealing drugs or running an escort service, or something similar. He's out.

Another prospective tenant may make $800 a month. That means she will not likely have enough for rent, which should only be 25 to 30 percent of one's monthly income. (However, this is rarely true: 30 to 40 percent of renters in the United States put almost 50 percent of their income into rent.) So she's out.

You can also ask, "How much do you make a week?" The answer: "I make $400." If the rent is $400 a month, that ratio appears to work. But it's better to ask the question this way: "How much do you bring home a week?" If the answer is $285 and the rent is $400, that amount won't cover the rent. So be sure to ask the right questions.

By screening prospective tenants on the phone and asking questions to verify income, you rule out people who just cannot afford to live in your house or apartment.

Talk to Two Previous Landlords

In addition to a credit check and a criminal-background check, I talk with two of the applicant's previous landlords. Why two? Consider this: Joe is living in an apartment and hasn't paid rent to Bill, his landlord, in months. He tore up Bill's place and they got into a fistfight two weeks ago. So I call Bill and say, "Well, Joe is thinking about moving into my place. I have an empty house he wants to move into this week. Bill, what kind of recommendation would you give him?"

Bill thinks, "This is my chance to get rid of Joe," and he says, "Oh, Joe is the greatest. He pays the rent on time; he's a good guy. As a matter of fact, I am going to help him move. I have a pickup truck. We will load it up today and bring him over there." In other words, Bill would say *anything* to get Joe out of his property.

Dave was Joe's landlord before Bill was. Joe may have lived in Dave's place two years ago and torn it up and failed to pay rent. So be sure to contact Dave. Because Joe is not living in Dave's place now, Dave will more likely tell the truth than Bill, and will say, "Joe lived here and what a nightmare! Where is that so-and-so? We've got a collection against him." This shows why you should contact at least two previous landlords.

One time, I called a previous landlord's number and actually got a nine-year-old kid on the phone. He posed as an applicant's landlord. In answer to my questions, he said, "Yeah, I'm . . . she's . . . oh yeah, I'm supposed to say that!" This is what people try to get away with.

Verifying Employment

You also want to verify your prospective tenant's employment. If, after you have called previous employers, you find that person has given you inaccurate information, be sure to verify every fact before proceeding.

Make sure you (or your credit-checking service) verify employment for at least the past two years. If prospective tenants are self-employed, be extra careful. Ask to see their 1099s, their latest tax returns, and recent bank statements to confirm they actually do have a business and an income. Beware—about 75 percent of start-up entrepreneurial businesses fail in less than a year.

Screening Summary

Four screening points:

1. Screen your applicants on the phone first. If they get past the first questions ("Where do you live now? Where did you live? Why are you moving?), fill out the application at that point.
2. Verify the information (either yourself or through a credit-checking company) on the application as soon as possible.
3. Verify employment. If the applicant is self-employed, review 1099s, tax returns, and bank statements to make sure the business is a legitimate one.
4. Call at least two previous landlords. If you suspect they could be relatives of the applicant, take time to check them out and make sure they really are landlords.

Giving someone a key is a big deal, so don't do it until you have conducted a thorough credit check and a background check, have verified employment, and have talked with two previous landlords.

Minimum Requirements

While you are deciding who your targeted tenants will be, make a list of minimum requirements as part of your policies and procedures. The Fair Housing laws say you have to rent to the first person meeting your minimum requirements, so put these in writing or you risk getting into all kinds of trouble.

If you like Tom better than Sally, or you pick one applicant who is black over one who is white, or select a Catholic over a Muslim, the government can come after you for a Fair Housing violation. HUD pursues this regulation aggressively. You could ask that "the applicant must have had a steady job for three years" as one of your requirements; just make sure you don't base any requirement on race, creed, or color, as stated in the statutes. (Check with your local attorney about Fair Housing laws.)

Be careful about saying "no children" in your minimum requirements. Federal laws state you may not discriminate against prospective tenants on the basis of family status—whether they are married, unmarried, or have no children. Here are five suggested minimum requirements:

1. The person must have acceptable credit (that means whatever is acceptable to you—e.g., no late rent payments—above a certain credit score).
2. The person must pass the criminal-background check.
3. Establish a verifiable income that is a certain percent of the rent (use 25 or 35 percent or a percentage you feel comfortable with, but be sure to state a percentage).
4. A recommendation must be given by two previous landlords.
5. Tenants and their families must appear to be neat and polite. (Some people have had great credit and could pay the rent, but they were snotty and demanding, and they openly yelled at their kids. You clearly don't want these people in your properties.)

Fair Housing Laws

You cannot choose your tenants freely. Remember that Fair Housing laws prevent you from discriminating on the basis of race, religion, creed, color, ethnic origin, or disability. If both Joe and Charita

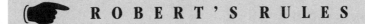

ROBERT'S RULES

Put all of your minimum rental requirements in writing. You must treat everyone the same and rent to the first person who meets those minimum requirements. This is not only good business practice, but it is also the law, according to the Fair Housing statutes.

have the same credit rating but you like Joe better than Charita and decide to rent to him, Charita could file a federal Fair Housing suit, saying, "I am a woman, I am black, and I have good credit. You should rent to me."

HUD does test landlords, including myself. Testers call the number given in rental ads to see how landlords screen prospective tenants. So protect yourself by putting your minimum requirements in writing and complying with the law. Then, if anyone questions your decision or you are tested, say, "That applicant didn't meet my minimum requirements." If somebody has a disability and uses a wheelchair but says he will pay for your place to become wheelchair accessible, you must rent to that person. You are not required to spend $9,000 to put in a ramp, but if the tenant is willing to pay for it, you have to oblige.

Credit-Denial Letters

Landlording can get complicated. I have learned that if you turn someone down for credit reasons, you may have to notify them by letter, according to the law. Consult your lawyer to verify what you have to do if you turn someone down due to poor credit. You would send an official letter stating that he or she didn't meet the minimum credit requirements. The person can follow up by getting a copy of his or her credit report to see where problems lie.

Some landlords have spent thousands of dollars in lawyers' fees when defending themselves on violations that are questionable. So keep it clean; get everything in writing; don't violate Fair Housing regulations; and don't do anything that even looks like a violation. I have been tested; you might be, too.

Occupancy Limits

There is a lot of discussion about how many people can legally reside in a place. The rules keep changing; everybody gets confused. There used to be a HUD rule: two people to a bedroom. It has been replaced by one limiting the number of people per square foot. (If you run up against this, I guarantee that if a family with six kids has lived in a two-bedroom apartment, you will not get good recommendations from previous landlords. So have people/square footage rules in your minimum requirements.) Check with your local attorney or your local landlord association.

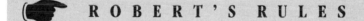

R O B E R T ' S   R U L E S

I constantly consult with local attorneys who know Fair Housing and landlord/tenant laws. They review my company's policies, procedures, documents, and forms. This small cost that prevents disputes has saved me hundreds of thousands of dollars later on.

CHAPTER 6

Moving Tenants In

Home is the place where, when you go there, they have to take you in.

–Robert Frost

You have advertised your property, you have handled phone calls from people wanting to see the property, and you have set rents. You have screened applicants on the phone and in person, and collected application fees. The applicants have passed all your tests and are ready to move in.

In the process of being a landlord, my philosophy (and I hope yours, too) is to always treat tenants like valued customers. Therefore, my goal is to have the place ready and perfect when they move in. At the beginning, they are excited about moving in. But if something doesn't work, they call with complaints, their attitude crashes immediately, and they certainly don't feel like they've been treated as valued customers.

A Move-In Inspection

I want to eliminate any need for phone calls, back and forth, that become time-consuming and aggravating for everybody—and that cost money. So, using a move-in inspection (see the sample Move-In Inspection form in Appendix B), we go through the place and check things out. If something doesn't work, we fix it now, not later.

As a landlord, you should also have a Management Move-In Checklist (see the sample in Appendix D). It covers the application and verification forms filled out, the deposit received, the first month's rent, the security deposit, the move-in payment, the rental agreement, and additional agreements. Be sure to document everything. What gets documented gets done. On the inspection form we use, we ask tenants to initial each item and sign the form. If, at move-out time, they say, "That hole in the wall and that black stain on the carpet were there when I moved in," you can refer to the list they signed. If it wasn't noted at the beginning of the lease period, the tenants are responsible for repair costs.

It is best to have tenants go through the inspection with you, for two reasons: (1) So you deal with any problems right away; and (2) so there is no disagreement at the end of the leasing term about the condition of the place at the start. This determines whether tenants get back their security deposit when they move out, so it's in their best interest to work with you on this. (See the sample Security Deposit Policy statement in Appendix C.)

Give tenants all the paperwork they need at the move-in, including a form for requesting repairs. Then explain your inspection procedure. I recommend you inspect once a month or at least every 45 days; that communicates to the tenant that you care. Also, if there's some foul play that affects your property, you will find out about it. And it's good for tenants to see that you're around. When renters think you're not around, they are more likely to let things go. We make a big deal about these inspections. Some landlords believe you should never let your tenants see you because they will ask you to fix this or replace that. I have the opposite point of view, which says, "We care; this is our business. We are here and you know we are here." That way, if tenants behave badly (e.g., they're dealing drugs or 15 people are crashing there), we won't let that go on for months. We know within 30 days.

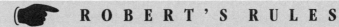

ROBERT'S RULES

Take care of maintenance and repair items now rather than later. If you don't, tenants will complain, they will balk at paying the rent, and they will find more repairs that need to be done. All of a sudden, your good relationship becomes questionable. Fix whatever is broken now, so you don't have to fix a broken relationship later.

Inspecting Your Properties

Conduct inspections of all your properties every 30 to 60 days. (See the sample Monthly Inspection Report for Month of . . . in Appendix B.) Make it part of your policies and procedures. Whether you have a no-fault maintenance plan or a deductible one (explained in Chapter 8), be aware of any problems, so you can fix them or get the tenant to handle them before the problems become serious.

By inspection, I don't mean going through the place with a white glove, as one would in a military barracks. You can learn a lot by just pecking your head in the door. We go in and spray for bugs every month, and we change furnace and air conditioner filters. We let the tenant know, in writing, when the inspection will be conducted. (Never go into a place without giving the tenants notice in writing.)

At the move-in, we have already given them a note telling them we come in on the second Tuesday of every month to spray for bugs and to inspect. That's the time when we walk around with the bug-spray guy and just look. We leave behind a door-hanger notice, so they know we came by. Also, this lets us in on what is happening in the neighborhood. I challenge every landlord to do this consistently: If you don't inspect, you won't like the surprises you will get.

Also, you will probably give your tenants a lead-based-paint disclosure form and booklet if your place was built before 1978. They have to sign a release form—that is a federal law. You incur a substantial fine—$10,000—if you don't present your tenants with this document and have them sign it.

In addition to the lead-based-paint disclosure, I send another letter, which tells the tenant he or she is "renting a place that was built before 1978," and that "it may have lead-based paint." Therefore, the tenant understands the risk and what he or she is doing. (See the sample Disclosure of Information on Lead-Based Paint in Appendix C.)

I put this signed letter in the file-folder I keep for a tenant, so if a lawsuit for lead-based paint comes up, and if I do not have the signed disclosure form and proper insurance on it, I do have another letter that says these people knew what they were doing. You can get the form from your local HUD office; it is a federal law concerning not only property built before 1978, but also any property you know that may have lead-based paint in it.

Some landlords have a rule: Never go into a rental property without at least two people. I have never had a problem with sending only one—probably because we do a criminal-background check and a credit check on everyone, not just tenants, but anyone we employ, including most contractors. Remember that if you allow known criminals into your tenants' homes and they steal something while there, you will be held liable.

Making Tenants Your Friends

As a landlord, you can be as personal, friendly, and loving toward your tenants as you want to be. Some landlords believe we should never get familiar with our tenants or even call them by their first names. They believe if you develop a rapport with them, they will want to be your friend, and yet one day you might have to evict them.

Others take the opposite viewpoint and recommend that you become friends. They believe that when tenants like you, they'll stay longer. I tend to stand somewhere in between these extremes; I am a friendly landlord but I always remember that we have a business relationship, so I don't get too involved with them. I simply want my rent and my properties taken care of. In return, tenants want a place to live and things taken care of when they need repairs or replacements. It is one of the simplest business relationships that exists—I encourage you to remember that.

As the landlord, you get to set the rules in this relationship. If you don't, your tenants will. So tell them everything: your office hours; where you are; when and how to pay rent; and how to ask for repairs. Be strict about that, so you remain in control.

In addition to making sure everything in the place works, connect with your new tenants within the first ten days after they move in. I do two things: (1) I send them a personal letter (see the sample Welcome Letter in Appendix B) or I call and ask if everything is okay; and (2) after a few more days, I call again and say, "We are glad you moved in; welcome to the neighborhood. Is everything okay there now?" Don't let time go by without making a connection.

Rules and Regulations

With the lease, you should also have a list of rules and regulations that spell out what you expect from your tenants. Make a big deal about telling the tenant to review and sign this list; any violation of these rules is a violation of the lease and becomes grounds for eviction.

Also, receiving your rent on time is important. I often have new tenants handwrite, on a sheet of paper, the date when they will pay. For example, they might write, "I promise to pay the rent by the third of the month." Then they would sign it and give it to me. That way, they cannot say they didn't know the policy, even though it was stated in the lease (see the sample lease in Appendix C).

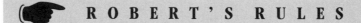

ROBERT'S RULES

I believe that if all contracts were handwritten, there would be fewer court cases because it's easy to prove something that is stated in the tenant's handwriting. Then there can be absolutely no doubt about what we agreed on. We have a good lease prepared by our attorney, but I think that all leases are only as good as the integrity of the people who sign them.

Four Absolutes for Your Lease

Be sure to include in your lease these four items: First, tenants are responsible for their own security, which is becoming a big deal right now. Second, if there is a dispute that has to go to court, they are responsible for their own attorney's fees. (Note: If you don't have a lease or if your lease doesn't include that provision, you usually cannot get the attorney's fees from your tenants and you might have to sue for fees after the fact.) Third, the lease should include the date when the rent is due. Fourth, include the term of the lease. I usually do only one-year leases, but if someone requests it, I will give a two-, three-, or four-year lease.

Generally, we sign two-year, three-year, and five-year leases. Some landlords offer a six-month lease. On a month-to-month arrangement, in most states, you could raise the rent every month after giving 30 days' notice. If you lease for a year, you cannot raise the rent unless you have an automatic increase included in the lease. If you do a lease for more than a year, be sure to have an automatic rent increase built in. Always increase the rent regularly to keep up with inflation. (I also include some clauses about rent collection and no-fault maintenance, which are discussed in Chapter 8.) Have tenants sign the lease and give them a copy when you give them the door key. Remind your tenants that if they lose their key, they must pay to replace it.

I suggest you deal up front with the two biggest complaints landlords have about renters—collecting rents and dealing with damages. Be sure to communicate the policies and procedures you use in writing. (See the sample Late Fees Due Notice and the sample Pay Rent or Quit Letter in Appendix B.) For example, your policy might state that the rent is due on the 1st of the month and late on the 5th. We evict on the 12th if rent is not paid by then.

Let tenants know you are serious. If they fail to pay by the 12th, file eviction papers. (See the sample for the 30 Days' Notice to Terminate Tenancy in Appendix B.) Also, know that if you let the due date go by for one tenant and not another, you could be hauled into court for discrimination.

Some prospective tenants who passed my inspection told me, "I can't pay all the rent by the 10th or the 11th. I only get paid this much and I have all these bills." When you hear something like that, don't move the person in; it is not worth it. Just shake the person's hand and say, "This isn't going to work. Good-bye and good luck." Again, use your common sense to decide.

 R O B E R T ' S   R U L E S

Think about your business this way. If you have a mortgage with a bank and you miss your payment deadline, you will definitely receive a late notice, then a foreclosure notice. Bank officers do not care about your problems; they are paid to enforce the bank's policy. You might care about your tenants and sympathize when they have problems, but you also have a business to run and policies and procedures to follow. Stick to them.

Word gets around. If Steve is a landlord who lets his tenants pay a little on Friday and a little next week, he will fill his places with people who like to pay a little at a time. If Mary lets drug dealers in, guess what most of her tenants end up being!

On the other hand, if you are tough and you show it with your actions, by evicting on the stated date, most of your tenants will pay the rent on time or certainly by the stated eviction date. They know that if they don't, you will evict them.

Never Accept Cash

In terms of collecting rents in cash, I have a strict policy: I do not accept cash from anybody. A lot of landlords like cash because it's handy and they may not report all of their rental-property income to the IRS. But I would recommend that you refuse to accept cash because of thievery. If I walk around with $1,000 in my pocket and if people know I am collecting rent, at some point I am going to be robbed. Criminals know where cash is. Also, because I have staff on the premises, I don't want cash lying around in case it gets stolen. We manage 350 places from our office, so we keep a big sign, in an obvious location, that says, "No cash." If tenants walk into the office with cash, we tell them to get a money order and bring the funds back. We do not touch cash.

By contrast, a landlord who has an office down the street from our office manages 300 properties and has a bulletproof glass window, so tenants can pay their rents on the premises. He has installed cameras and put big locks on his doors. But he has been robbed four times in 12 months. It's because he has $8,000 to $12,000 in cash in the office at any one time, and word gets around.

We don't even accept rent in our office anymore. If someone walks into it, we say, "Please mail that to our accounting department" (which is us, of course). "Here is the post office box address." With a lot of drug addicts living in our communities, cash has become a dangerous medium. I prefer to handle rents strictly by checks, money orders, and post office boxes.

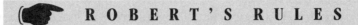

ROBERT'S RULES

I have so many stories to tell about confrontations with tenants in my early years of landlording. I have been chased and threatened, and have had bottles thrown at me. One lady once came at me with a stick. Now, if someone is unhappy or yells at me, I simply leave or hang up the phone. I don't get paid enough to listen to people yell and scream. I write a note that says, "Whatever you need, give us a call and leave the information on the voice mail or send me a note with your complaint." Don't get caught up in confrontations; they are unnecessary.

First One to Pay Gets the Place

Here's another hard-earned lesson I learned. I used to pick up the phone and hear, "Yes, I want to rent the apartment on 100 Jones Street. That is perfect for me, been dreaming of it all my life. I will be there Monday; hold it for me, I just have to have it!" Then I turned away other callers because I thought I'd rented it to the first caller—but she didn't show up. So now I say, "The first person who is qualified, and shows up with the money, wins." I suggest keeping the activity going until someone hands you deposit money.

When it comes to accepting an initial payment of the first month's rent as a deposit, be sure to write on the receipt: "This holds the property until [the date shown]." If the prospective tenant doesn't show up by then, this money covers damages for lost time and lost rent. If you don't have that provision written specifically in large print where it's easily understood, the courts in your state (laws differ from state to state) might not allow you to keep that deposit. So spell out the terms in writing and hope it clears up all questions in the future: "If you don't come back Tuesday with the rest of the rent and fulfill the contract, you lose this money."

Realize that security deposits are not *your* money, but the tenant's money. In many states, you are required to hold deposits in an escrow account; in some states, you cannot even earn interest on the deposited funds. And in some states, you must give the tenant in writing, and item by item, the reasons that you are keeping the deposit— that is the law. Most states require you to give it to them within 30 days, after they have moved out.

You are supposed to keep a separate bank account for security deposits, in almost every state. I want to be very clear about that. What I like about a lease-option situation is that it doesn't require a security deposit, which is not your money; it requires option money, which *is* yours (see Chapter 11 for details).

Move-In Summary

Here are three points to keep in mind:

1. Inspect the properties and fix any maintenance problems before you let new tenants move in. (My goal is to have them move in and to stay for 25 years or 30, so my mortgages get paid off.)
2. Hand the new tenants a copy of all the rules and regulations and the lease (see samples in Appendix C). Make sure they understand what is written in the lease.
3. Include a letter recommending that tenants buy the Renters Insurance policy. For less than $200 or so a year, they are covered in case of theft, fire, and other damages. In the lease, make it clear that you are not responsible for those details.

CHAPTER 7

Collecting All of the Rent, All of the Time

If your ship doesn't come in, swim out to it.

–Jonathan Winters

If you have tenants who always pay their rent on time, you have truly great tenants. The fact remains, however, that a lot of renters pay their rent late. If you charge $500 a month for rent and charge a 10 percent late fee after the 5th of the month, your renter owes $550. But what really happens? If Ms. Smith sends you $500 on the 6th, your next move is to send her a letter or call her and say, "Ms. Smith, you have to pay a late fee." She will protest or ask for a special favor or say it's not right, or something else. Face the fact that you are going to have trouble collecting late fees.

Rent Discounts

Here's a better solution using a different psychology. Tell Ms. Smith, "Your rent is $550 but if we receive it on or before the 1st of the month, we will give you a $50 discount." That sounds much better than a late fee, because nobody likes to be penalized; everybody likes to be rewarded. Hand out candy, not penalties.

Let's take this idea a step further. If a tenant has paid late before, it's probable that he or she will pay late again so, to preempt that, send a letter that says, "If you are late next month, here is what you owe and here are the penalties. You will be evicted if you don't comply." If you have problem tenants, deal with them. Don't wait for them to be late again and drag it out for another 15 days. (See the sample letter for the Late Fees Due Notice in Appendix B.) If the problem persists, you will want to send a stronger letter, such as a Pay Rent or Quit Letter (see three options for this kind of letter in Appendix B).

You can get even more aggressive and charge an additional 10 percent per day (or whatever increment you choose). However, be aware that some states have late-fee limitations. In some areas, it may be illegal when you start charging a $100 late fee on a rent of $500. Again, the courts are all over the place. Some require ten days' notice before landlords can evict tenants. I find that our discounted-rent program—rent is due on the 25th, late on the 1st, with eviction occurring ten days later—sounds and looks better than late fees. People get excited if they can save money.

If the law in your state says late fees cannot be charged unless rents are five days late, make rents due on the 25th or 25th of the previous month. That way, rent is already late on the 1st or the 2nd. Also, the courts have ruled that (assuming there's no other statement) if something has been mailed by a specified date, it is considered sent. So you want to put in the lease "received by" a particular day to enforce your deadlines. It's amazing how many times you hear, "Well, I mailed it!" We say, "We didn't receive it.," The tenant says, "But the check really is in the mail."

In most cases, if you mail a letter to a local address on one day, it should arrive the next—in two days at the most. Meanwhile, many times I can't get hold of my renters. I try to call or drive by, and they're not there. It's best to write a letter, put it in the mail, and know they will have it soon. Use large print and simple language. Don't fuss and fume when all you have to do is send your message through the post office.

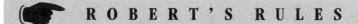

ROBERT'S RULES

If a tenant says, "I get paid on the 18th; can I pay my rent on the 18th instead of on the 1st?," I always say no to these requests because of recordkeeping. If you run your business by having to keep track of who pays when, it gets out of hand. Keep it simple and consistent for everyone. Stick to your policies and procedures.

Keeping Rent Rolls

Whether you collect rent from one tenant or from ten or from a hundred, you need a Rent Roll System. You can set it up on a computer—using accounting, spreadsheets, and property management software—or you can do it as some successful landlords do, on paper. You don't have to be sophisticated about this.

On the Rent Roll, we list the property address and the tenant's name and phone number (in case we need to call the person urgently); the amount of the rent; and then we have a column for the amount paid, the time, and the date. That's how you keep track of the rent.

Tracking Systems

On any day, a good landlord needs to be able to look at a sheet of paper and tell what percentage of the rent has been collected to date. This should be true no matter how many properties you handle. You need to know, every day, what percentage of the rent came in, and whether it is on a handwritten sheet or on a computer. Quick-Books Pro® does that for us, but many other software programs can handle this.

☞ R O B E R T ' S   R U L E S

I want to stress the importance of writing down all your rental procedures. Many landlords are "single gunslingers" who like to do everything themselves. But what if they get hurt or disappear for three weeks, or even win the lottery? Someone should be able to walk into your office, look at the paperwork, and figure out rents, due dates, amounts, and the place to deposit checks. I recommend you set up a management book that anyone, including yourself, can follow. You also need the book for yourself so that you don't forget anything.

You also want to know your expenses, your vacancies, and your rents. Set up a tickler file to know when leases are up, so you can get a rent increase. The law in many states requires you to give tenants 30 days' or 60 days' notice when the rent is going up. You cannot just casually tell renters, "The lease is up October 1st and your rent is going up." You are required to inform your tenants in advance. Check with the landlord association and/or local attorneys on requirements in your area.

Weekly Rent Payments

You might consider collecting rents by the week. This comes with one big advantage: Let's say your duplex rents for $400 a month; but if you collect $100 every week for the same property, you actually collect an average of $433 a month—almost a 10 percent rent increase.

If you asked renters in the low- to moderate-income area how they would prefer to pay rent, they would say weekly because they get paid weekly or maybe biweekly. So offer a choice in their rental payment program. Simply say, "The rent is $400 a month, but we have a special program: If you want to pay weekly, it will be $125 a week." Because time is money, it will take more time to collect these rents. And you are giving them something they want—so get paid for it.

However, we don't want to visit tenants every Friday night to collect their rents. Although we discourage them from coming to our office, we have set up a heavily fortified mailbox with a slit in front of it. Some people make arrangements with their banks to have the rent money dropped off. Alternatively, tenants can also mail it in every week. With weekly payments, evictions are fewer and delinquency is lower because people get paid weekly or biweekly.

With weekly renters, not only do we get that $33 rent increase, but we also charge them for it with a higher rent. Now, that difference may not seem like a lot, but I get an extra $25 a week, which amounts to $100 a month; plus, we get the extra $33 a month. So instead of receiving $400 a month, it adds up to about $550—an extra $1,700 a year for the same property. Multiply that by several units and you'll boost your income by thousands of dollars a year. I have so many units now that I may just pay somebody to manage the weekly rentals alone because they bring in so much more money.

You can implement this idea with biweekly rents but, again, charge for it. When people come in to rent from you, you say, "We have some special programs; how often do you get paid?" "Every two weeks." Then: "Would you like to try our twice a month program, at $250 for each payment?"

In addition to getting larger payments, your advantage is that a period of two weeks is the most their payments can get behind. When they pay by the month and pay late, they can get behind by two weeks, three weeks, or even more; and in reality, it often goes to 50 days before anything happens.

The disadvantage of weekly rentals, of course, is the added headache of collecting four payments a month instead of one.

Occasionally, people will pay rent in advance. In some cases, you can get three months' or four months' rent ahead of time—say when they get a lump-sum settlement or a tax refund. Of course, accept the offer and, if you are feeling generous, give them a discount for the pre-payment.

Group Rentals

At times you may be dealing with a group home situation, partic-ularly if you rent to students. If you have someone on your premises who is assigned, as a tenant trustee, to collect rent, be extra careful. In every situation I know of, either (1) the trustee runs off with the money at some point or (2) he or she starts giving breaks to friends and doesn't collect the right amounts. The reason is simple: A trustee's interest doesn't align with your interests, so it's best to col-lect the rent yourself. It will save you trouble. We prefer to have ten-ants put the rent check in the slot set up at the office or send it via mail. If they mail it on Friday or on Saturday, I will get it on Monday or Tuesday. If I don't have it by Tuesday, I am prepared to take action to collect it. That's simpler than working with a tenant trustee.

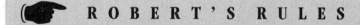

R O B E R T ' S   R U L E S

It is always best to have the rent mailed in. This will save you and your staff both time and money. Instead of hav-ing to deal with the daily or hourly interruptions involved in collecting rent, someone can just process the incoming mail. If you give out preprinted envelopes and make them a bright color, they will attract the tenants' attention. We use bright-red, preprinted envelopes, so the tenants can easily see them sitting on a desk or table.

"I'm Just the Manager"

Here's a collection technique we use when tenants ask for an exception to any of our policies. Our response is at least partly true: "I am so sorry, but I am just doing my job; the owner is a jerk! I wish the rent wasn't due on the first. But I am just the lowly management guy." Always present yourself as being on the tenant's side of the issue. Now, I can do that because I am a Gemini and have a split personality. I can also say, "The rent goes to the post office box and the Accounting Department. I cannot stand those people. They insist that the rent must be mailed in, and that you have to pay all these late fees and penalties. They are jerks. I am with you 100 percent; I am on your side. So please don't wait any longer; pay that rent so they don't start throwing you out of here."

I am serious about this because we do have accountants and they can be jerks—and I am "they." But my tenants don't need to know that. I come across as the lowly manager. Oh, some people figure it out; they have contacted the local Property Deed Office or seen the tax records. They learn that I own the property. Still, I tell them the owner is a jerk and I say, "Even though I would love to make an exception, the owner won't let me."

The point behind these examples is that you segregate the rent collection function and procedures from yourself personally. Emotionally, it makes it easier for both you and the tenant. Simply say, "Rules are rules. I cannot stand them either, but that is how it is!"

Broken Leases

Suppose your tenants sign a one-year lease, stay for six months, and then decide to relocate, buy a house, and move out of the state. Can they legally break the lease? In most states, landlords have a duty to rerent the apartment. They have to advertise and promote it. So if it takes one month to rerent it, the outgoing tenant can only be charged for the one month of lost rent, plus any expenses associated with moving out.

The landlord could keep the security deposit but must document all expenses (such as documenting that rent cannot be collected for a month and a half). In most states, you are not allowed to collect a double rent on your property. You cannot collect from both parties at one time for the same property. That is the law in most states; please check with your local attorney.

When one of my tenants wants to move out before the end of the lease, I say, "Well, you signed a year's lease. You have only been here six months, so you owe us six months' rent. What do you propose we do?" Maybe the tenant offers the full amount; if so, take it. Maybe he or she offers two months' rent. That will probably cover expenses and lost rent until you can rerent it. But in any case, you should get paid *something;* you cannot just sign one-year or two-year leases and let people walk away from them without a penalty. Every time someone moves, it costs you between $800 and $1,200 dollars. Remember that this is a business.

Alternatives for Nonpayment

To collect rent when tenants don't pay on time, you can also work with collection attorneys, who take one-third of what they collect as their fee, as well as court costs. Assuming it's stated in the lease, tenants are charged for the court costs and the attorney's fees. When you turn the matter over to an attorney, it is marked on the tenant's credit report, so when the next prospective landlord pulls a report, it shows the tenant did not pay the last time. Also, when delinquent tenants want to buy a house or a condo, they have to have paid off the rent owed previously. If they get a job or a bank account, the collection attorney can also attach payment of their funds owed to their bank account or wages.

In my first years as a landlord, I commonly let people off the hook. Recently, however, I have been able to collect thousands of dollars from fleeing tenants I thought would never earn a dollar or come up with any money. Remember that judgments in most states are good for seven to ten years, and sometimes can even be renewed for another seven to ten years. They might not be able to pay you now, but they will pay you later. Sometimes you can even collect interest on the debt.

When the tenant cannot pay the rent, we send out a letter that says, "Here are some people who can help you with the rent because we don't want to have you evicted." The list includes government social agencies—most cities have programs to help renters with their rent—as well as churches, Big Brother organizations, and other charities. We help them by introducing them to these agencies. In my city, many agencies will give one month's rent (only once) to anybody who asks for it. (One agency is an organization in Nashville called Metro Action.) Most cities have similar programs.

A tenant called Eva got behind on four months' rent—about $2,000. Then Eva got busy contacting these agencies and raised $2,000 from churches, Big Brother groups, and social agencies. She gave it to me because she owed it to me. Now she works at a church and helps others who cannot pay their rent. She is living evidence that if people are willing to work at it, they can get results.

Alternatively, you can ask renters to sell something—a boat, a car, a television set, or a couch. Any of them could raise money to pay the rent. In most cases, if they really want to pay you, they can.

CHAPTER 8

Taking the Headaches Out of Maintenance

Never let work drive you; master it and keep it in complete control.

–Booker T. Washington

Maintenance can be a headache. Every time the phone rings, it costs money and causes aggravation. However, you can do many things to reduce the stress level and the cost of repairs.

The Appliance Business

Appliances are the most expensive area of maintenance you have. So get out of the appliance business. To buy or replace a refrigerator and stove, it would cost $500 to $700, or more. The cost of repair calls on appliances is high; maintenance calls run $75 to $100, and parts cost that much, too. In the beginning of my landlord career, I spent a fortune on appliances.

Then I followed my own advice: Know your customer. A lot of tenants don't expect to have a refrigerator and a stove. If places already have them, we charge an extra $25 or $30 a month. If tenants won't pay for them, we take them out. Or, if we don't want to take them out, we put in the lease that these appliances are on loan. If they break, we do not repair or replace them.

Providing window air conditioners can be a hassle. They leak and break; you will spend a fortune on them. If your places have central air-conditioning and heating, and water heaters, get good-quality systems with warranties on them, assuming you can and that it makes sense for you. Even get extended warranties because, when they break, they cost a lot of money to fix. Your profit on an average house or duplex is $2,000 to $3,000 a year. But if you have to replace these big items, your profit disappears.

Also, realize that your basic Homeowners Insurance policy on renters doesn't cover appliances unless they are stolen, damaged in a fire or flood, or vandalized. Renters can get Renters Insurance, but that covers only *their* appliances.

The bottom line is: Get out of the appliance business if you can. And if you have to stay in it, at least get paid for it. Some landlords buy used appliances that cost $180 and they rent them for $30 a month; so in six months they are paid for, and bring in profits after that. Or you can take the next step—buy new, high-quality appliances, charge for them, and have a warranty. So know your tenants; know your market. That will determine how you handle appliances.

When tenants own their own appliances, they can tear up the floors when bringing them in and out of the place. In our low- to moderate-income property, we like to install that indestructible tile in the kitchens and bathrooms, the kind they use in school hallways. Most brands are reasonably priced and the flooring will last forever. It costs a little more to put it in, but you don't have to replace it every year, as you do with vinyl. It is worth the extra amount to put something in that lasts several years.

The Repair Business

Ask any landlord: repairs will eat you up. They take away all of your cash flow. Carpet: $800; broken faucets and plumbing: $50, $100, $200. Your whole month's profit could literally be flushed down the toilet. And repairs steal your time. Also, some repair calls are just not real, nothing is wrong; we go out and find the sink isn't leaking and the toilet works fine.

Here's another example. A utility company's program subsidized my costs for putting central heating and air-conditioning into some of my units. They gave me a favorable interest rate, insulated the units, and put central air and heat—brand new equipment—into some duplexes. After they were installed, my maintenance line kept ringing off the hook (that's when I used to answer it myself) and Ms. Smith, for example, called to say, "It is hot out and I have no air-conditioning; it doesn't work." After all the effort and expense of the past few days, this made me really upset. So I drove to her place and, sure enough, the temperature in the apartment was 99 degrees. Ms. Smith didn't know she had to switch the setting to on. When I flipped the switch to on, all of a sudden, we had cool air. It's best to avoid spending your time that way.

Other times, a tenant would call and say, "My smoke detector doesn't work." Then I learned the kids took the batteries out to put into their Walkmans. Whenever we go out to troubleshoot, it costs money, so having a deductible avoids these kinds of "emergencies."

To help you avoid dealing with false alarms and getting out of the maintenance business, here are two suggestions: no-fault maintenance and deductibles. (Note: These may or may not be legal in your area or they may not apply if you are managing a large complex.)

No-Fault Maintenance

Consider offering a no-fault maintenance program, especially if you rent to someone who is good at doing minor repairs. Say that "you can save a lot of money by taking care of the repairs yourself. For a rent reduction of $15, $20, or $30 a month and no-fault maintenance, you take care of the minor repairs yourself. You are not responsible for the roof or the hot-water heater, the major items. But up to the first $100 or $200, you pay it. If we pay the repair cost up front, we add the cost to your rent."

A lot of renters like this program and so do landlords, especially if you have already started negotiating from a higher rent. Remember the example of asking prospective tenants how much they wanted to pay and they said $475, or $50 higher than the rent price of $425 I had set? In this case, I follow up by saying, "How would you like to save $30 a month off that?"

Before you offer this, however, remember to do two things: First, make sure the tenants actually do the repairs. If they let the sink leak for six months and don't fix it, you have a $2,000 floor problem. Second, be sure to inspect the place periodically. If you see they haven't fixed anything in two months and the place is falling apart, then you may need to renegotiate the contract. If you don't check for a year, you are likely to find a soft board in the kitchen where they never fixed the leak; a broken door or window; or something much worse. Use a monthly inspection form and inspect your properties faithfully.

When landlords lease a commercial space, tenants take care of repairs. We also apply that principle to homes and duplexes. In some states, that may not be legal—the law may not allow you to opt out of fixing rental units, so find out. If Housing Department inspectors come around and see things in disrepair, they will hold the landlord responsible for completing repairs, so be aware of that.

Deductibles

A lot of insurance products come with a deductible—if you want your car fixed, for example, you have to spend the first $500. You can use the same principle with your rental agreement. The landlord pays for a repair but the tenant pays the first $50 of the repair cost. That takes care of about 75 percent of the repairs—the leaky sinks, the doorknobs replaced, and the screens fixed. Have your tenants sign an agreement about this deductible, making sure they understand it and initial it. When they call and request a repair of a leaking sink, say that "we will be more than glad to send Joe out there, but remember that you have a deductible. It will cost you $50." Be sure to enforce this agreement.

If you have a record of being soft, your tenants will likely protest or deny they knew they were supposed to pay. Stay firm and don't send the message that you won't stick to anything—on-time rent payments and evictions. Treat landlording as a business and you will avoid nightmares. This is the real world.

Damage

Very rarely have I found when something is damaged, that the damage was my fault. Landlords are responsible for taking care of wear and tear but not for willful damage, negligence, and stupidity. So charge tenants for their damage; charge them for having you try to fix things they damaged. As the owner, you are ultimately responsible for fixing damages, such as a clogged toilet or sink. If we don't do essential repairs, we could receive a letter from HUD and have a lot of hassle when dealing with an infraction. Our policy is to add the cost of fixing damages to their rent. We make it clear that if they don't pay it, they get evicted—that is just business.

Yet most landlords don't even charge their tenants for damage, justifying it by saying, "These people have been here for two years. Spending $80 to fix this place isn't much. I will let them off this time." But that is still $80. Why walk away from it? Repeated spending of it over many months, and for many units, adds up to a lot of money over time. So charge for repairs, document the activity, and make sure you get paid.

In my experience, the worst purveyors of letting damage payments go are landlords involved in public housing for low-income renters. Over the years, many tenants who left the "projects" rented from us. When I objected to their damaging my property and I tried to charge them for it, they were just baffled. They'd even say, "We used to tear our apartments up and not have to pay for it—why should we have to pay for it here?" That's another reason to stick with your policies and procedures.

Preventive Measures

This all relates to "training" your tenants. Just as you would do with children or employees, if you select good people to start with and communicate your expectations, they will behave well. If you don't screen and train your tenants, you pay the price of having them damage your property. Charge for repairs and let them know the charges up front. Make repairs a profit center—for example, if it costs you $50 to unclog the toilet, charge $85 or $100. They pay for the time and aggravation as well as the hard costs. Remember that every business gets paid for time and aggravation.

If a tenant claims that "this neighbor kid threw a rock in the window, and we want you to fix it," I encourage them to own up to their responsibility in the matter. Tenants can behave like kids: "I didn't do it! Wasn't me!" Impress on them that it is their home and they are responsible for everything that goes on in that home. If you let a kid in and he breaks a window, you are still responsible. I can say, "I will be more than happy to help you collect the funds from the kid's parents next door. But you have to pay now to get the window fixed."

 R O B E R T ' S   R U L E S

Always charge tenants for damage. When they move in, have them sign a repair expense sheet that explains how much certain repairs will cost to fix; then diligently charge for those costs. For example, if they break a screen, it will cost them $50. If they clog the toilet and your plumber charges $50, charge them $90. If someone damaged your brand new car, you would make them pay for it—right? The same goes for your rental properties.

Criminal Activities

When something happens, put a statement in your policies and procedures about criminal activities and don't hesitate to call the police. If tenants are throwing rocks, threatening you, tearing up the unit, or writing bad checks, these are real crimes. Call the police.

Sometimes I drive by my properties on the weekends, late at night, to see what is going on. It is amazing—a place that looks quiet on Friday afternoon, or at 11 in the morning, all of a sudden becomes lively on Saturday evening. That's when all the drug dealers and criminals tend to show up.

One time, I was driving by one of my properties and saw one of my tenant's kids throwing a brick at an apartment I owned. He sat in front of that building and kept throwing these bricks against the front door. I hollered from my car, then chased him (I was even on crutches, having undergone knee surgery), and actually caught him. (Pretty sad when a crippled man can catch a young kid.) I told him that damaging property is a crime and that I would be calling the police. When I talked with the police, I learned that this boy was already wanted on some other felony. Now he is in the juvenile court.

His mother said she would pay to replace the damaged door, but she never did—she got evicted. Still, if I don't take action, I know that word gets around. People think they can do whatever they want. So in this case, if I hadn't taken action, I know that word would have gotten around. "The landlord could charge but he doesn't." Again, business is business. Set policies and procedures, let people know, and enforce them consistently.

Emergencies

Be calm about how you define emergencies. I have been landlording for seven years and I have never had an emergency. I have been called to a fire or two, but I cannot do anything about them except

---

☞ **R O B E R T ' S   R U L E S**

Follow rules and regulations spelled out in the lease, being sure to attach all costs for damages to rent owed. Attach late fees, too. These become part of the rent and any unpaid rent can lead to eviction.

---

call the Fire Department. If criminal dealings take place on my property, I cannot do anything about them except call the police.

Even when pipes at a property broke at 3:00 AM, I knew that no plumber would go out until the next morning, so there was nothing to do until then. For many, these "emergencies" cause worry. I say, "Instead of worrying, do something about it. And if you cannot do anything about it, then don't worry about it."

Here's an example. I own five duplexes that are located next to each other. A few years ago, they got rocked by tornadoes. One day, I was talking to a tenant there—in the days when I used to chat on the phone with my tenants—and she said, "They fixed my sink the other week, but my doorknob is still loose."

And I said, "Okay, Ms. Smith, we will come by and fix it. How is everything else?"

"Great. The kids have been good. I don't like the neighbors much, though . . . . Oh, and by the way, the Fire Department is here next door. Your building is on fire; there are 30-foot flames coming out of it." Only after talking for 20 minutes about the weather and such did she tell me my building was shooting flames. However, I waited till the next day to go over there. I wasn't a fireman; there was nothing I could do.

As landlords, we don't have to drop everything and panic. We can reach people by mail; they will get our letters soon enough. At our company, we set up systems that help us stay calm. We have voice mail and check it the first thing in the morning and at about six in the evening. If people call at 11:00 at night or at 2:00 in the morning, we get the messages the next day. Nothing bad has ever happened because of this delay. In fact, if I had received the call at home at 1:00 AM, I doubt I would have dealt with it at that hour, anyway.

A pipe that bursts can do a lot of damage to a place. But if that happens and your property gets ruined, you have insurance to cover costs. Simply take care of situations in the best way you can. If you think about emergencies and feel stressed about them, you deal with a lot of worry—but that doesn't have to happen.

Maintenance Summary

Here are six points to keep in mind:

1. Explain the no-fault maintenance plan up front, in writing.
2. Have a three-day repair guarantee.
3. Return all phone calls within 24 hours.
4. Communicate your policies and procedures regarding maintenance.
5. Hand tenants expense sheets—which they sign to verify they've read them—listing specific costs for repairing each item: a broken screen, $40; a lockout key, $25.
6. Make everything a profit center: If the screen costs $20 to replace, charge $40. Time is money. Does an auto body shop charge only its cost for a part you need? No, it increases the cost significantly. So do the same with your business.

CHAPTER 9

Keeping Good Tenants

Do unto others as you would have them do unto you.

—The Golden Rule

Every day your property lies vacant, you lose rent money and increase your costs, repairs, and maintenance. If you had it rented for, say, $300 a month, your loss of income would be $10 a day. On top of that, you have to cover taxes, insurance, and interest on your mortgage. Plus, your unit is more likely to be vandalized when it's vacant. Just by being left empty, it could deteriorate and start to smell.

The Cost of Vacancies

Vacancies also cost in terms of time. You have to drive back and forth to show the unit, spend time on the phone, and meet with potential tenants. All of a sudden, your loss of $10 a day turns into a loss of $30 or $40 or more, depending on how you value your time.

To prevent tenants from leaving, set up a Tenant Retention Program that is based on how you treat them—a theme throughout this book and throughout business.

Your retention program should address things like returned phone calls, repair policies, Christmas cards, holiday gifts, and birthday greetings. For example, in some low-income areas, we give parties once a year or bring in meals. Sometimes we send our tenants discount-coupon booklets.

We also provide rewards when they move in and make a big deal about renewing leases by giving them gifts: a ceiling fan, a brass kickplate, or a carpet cleaning. They not only make the tenants happy, but they also increase the value of the property. I've created a win–win situation, rather than sponsoring a give-away. Some landlords go even further and say, "It you stay two years, or three, we will give you the refrigerator, or the stove, or a free trip. Or pay the rent on time, and we will give you $500." Do other companies reward their good customers? Of course, earning frequent flier points on the airlines is just one example.

In addition to rewards, devise a bonus program. For example, if the tenants stay the full year, they receive a ceiling fan; the second year, a new refrigerator; and the third year, $300. If you bought the property at the right price and have been collecting the rent faithfully, you can afford to give $300 to a tenant who has stayed three years. In fact, you have probably saved $1,800 in that time.

If you really want to keep the tenants you have, offer incentives. You could say, "You have been paying rent for two years, faithfully and on time. We will take $100 off the first month's rent if you sign another one-year lease." You don't want your tenants to leave—especially the good ones. With this program, you have that carrot when the rent is late. You'd say, "You know our bonus program? You are going to blow it." This sounds simple, but the programs are basic marketing tools that most landlords rarely use. And they work.

You could even have a monthly contest and give a $550 award to the tenant judged to have kept his or her unit the "nicest" for that month. That means keeping it in good repair and passing all inspections. When we offered this prize, it became a big deal. The tenants in the complex would compete fiercely for it. The cost can pay off in goodwill, in creating pride for having a well-kept home for the tenant, and in lowering long-term maintenance for the owners.

As a standard activity, we periodically send out letters to remind people about our maintenance line for repairs; we mention when the rent is due and tell them how much we appreciate them. Keeping contact with your tenants is important and profitable.

Referral Fees

Referral fees motivate people to ask around. Because of this, you will hear from people who are comfortable in the neighborhood because they already know someone living there.

Offering a $25 referral fee can be worthwhile if it saves you from having an empty unit. Assuming a rental income of $10 a day, you will have made back that $25 in fewer than three days. To get referrals, your flyer should say something like, "Do you know a good person looking for a clean, attractive place to live? We pay a referral fee. Call this number."

In my business, one tenant was such a great customer that we sought her help to attract more people like her. Now about eight people, who are all her friends, live on this one street. It's like a church picnic having them as tenants; they are honest and pay their rents on time. Realize that most people associate with others like themselves. So if you find someone who is a responsible tenant, encourage him or her to locate more tenants of similar quality.

Amazingly, if you treat people well, you will attract more tenants who will say, "He/she is a good landlord. I'm happy to send people there." These tenants become your best sources of referrals. So let your best tenants know when you have a unit available. But be careful—you don't want them to be the ones to move. Our policies don't allow a tenant move from one of our places to another because it creates a new vacancy.

Tenants Who Maintain Their Own Places

Our company doesn't offer an incentive for people to do their own maintenance work (unless it's part of an established program of rewards, or part of the no-fault program explained in Chapter 8). A lot of tenants might want to have their places painted after two years, so we buy the paint if they can paint themselves. I'm careful that they agree to paint walls a neutral color—not black or red or dark green. I made that mistake once and a tenant painted her walls black. It took us 18 coats to paint over it.

If I screen people and find out they've never painted before, I will not hand over a bucket of paint. But I have some tenants with experience—some even work professionally as painters. In general, though, we don't let tenants do work on our property unless we know their abilities.

 R O B E R T ' S   R U L E S

Use common sense and your best judgment when tenants request upgrades and repairs. If you always say no to the requests you receive, your tenants may move. And when they do, it costs at least $1,000 and plus, you may have lost great tenants. So you make the best business decision to keep your customers happy.

Remember, the biggest and best retention measure is to treat your clients right and to return their phone calls. If you do these things, you are considered exceptional. I guarantee you that if you return phone calls within 24 hours, make repairs within three days, take care of your tenants, and treat them fairly and cordially, you will rank close to the top 5 percent of all landlords.

When They Want to Move Out

When your tenants call and say they are leaving, make it a point of discussing their planned move with them. That makes you exceptional, too. Most landlords and property management companies say, "Well, sorry to see you go. Drop the key off. See you around. Bye."

Make time to call or visit those people and talk about why they are leaving. Remember that you are watching $800 to $1,500 flying out of your pocket when they go, so at least find out why they are leaving.

We actually studied the numbers and, over two years, we have stopped more than half of our tenants from leaving because we can usually fix the problems they cite for leaving: "I am tired of living here and I don't like the ceiling fan." We say that "we will get you another one right away." Tenants say, "Our smoke detector hasn't worked in a couple of weeks" or "The sink has been leaking a little bit." We say, "We'll take care of that." Maybe the issue is their surroundings: "Oh, we don't like the neighbor's kid; he's been fighting with our kid. " We say that "we will send a letter to the neighbor, telling the parents to stop their child from bothering your kid." "Okay, that would be great. We'll stay."

Sometimes they have delusions: "You see, we really want a three- or four-bedroom apartment." We reply, "But you only make $1,000 a month, and you pay $350 here. Where are you going that you can find one for this price?" "You mean we can't get a three-bedroom for $300?" "No, they rent for about $800." "Oh, we didn't know that. I guess we're not leaving." So ask why and help them solve their problem.

Our company can solve those problems and keep good tenants at a much lower cost than it takes to replace them. So can yours.

However, if they definitely want to leave, ask if they know of anyone else looking for a place. They probably invite friends and relatives over, and one of them may be interested in the place. When you advertise in the newspaper, people from all over the community come from the best neighborhoods and the worst. They often have no idea about the location of your place. As a result, you get a lot of weird calls. But people who already know that area and like it—and especially those who have friends nearby—can be the prime sources of leads for finding new tenants.

So when a tenant declares the intention to move out of your property, take these three steps:

1. Visit with your tenant and overcome any objections you can, so they change their minds about moving.
2. Assuming they do have to move, ask if they know anyone who would be interested in their place. It sounds like a simple thing to do, but landlords rarely take time to do this.
3. Put a For Rent sign in the yard before tenants move out. Get the calls coming in at least three weeks before the place becomes empty. Cut down the amount of time your place is vacant from 30 days to 10, or even fewer.

Make flyers and distribute them in the neighborhood. Everyone has people visiting—friends, relatives, and coworkers—who might know somebody who is looking for a place.

 ROBERT'S RULES

Whenever tenants want to move, find out why. If you can convince them to stay, you will be saving somewhere between $800 and $2,000 in lost rent, in refurbishing costs, and in finding a new tenant—not to mention that you'll save a great deal of your own time.

Increasing the Rent

Let's say your tenants are renting a place for $500 a month and you want to raise the rent. What amount would be fair?

Here's a way to answer that question and to handle rent increases. Assuming you want to keep these tenants, send them a personalized letter that begins: "Dear Max, We are so glad you are staying with us, and we want to continue to have you as a tenant." Then we get into something called an "exchange theory"—if I want something from you, I better give you something. People respond well to that. The letter continues: "Remember our reward program? We are going to clean your carpet (or give you a ceiling fan) because you have been such a good tenant. It is a very valuable gift, and we are pleased to give it to you. Meanwhile, expenses are going up, as you know: taxes, insurance, inflation."

Use good psychology: If I say your rent is going up, you won't like it. If I tell you why it is going up, you will understand. You do the same thing with children; you don't just shout, "Quit sticking your hand on the stove." You say, "Don't stick your hand on the stove because it will burn you. We love you and don't want you to get hurt and have to go the doctor." People want to be given reasons for requests.

So the letter continues: "Your rent is going up because taxes, insurance, expenses are all going up, too. Your rent increase is $50. However, if you have a problem with that, please contact the office." (If you want a $25 increase, write $50 in the letter.)

Half of the people who receive the letter will do nothing; half will call you. But for the half who do nothing, you just got an extra $50 a month. And 50 times 12 months comes to $600 in a year. That's enough for a getaway weekend plus a wonderful dinner and new shoes—and with money left over.

Negotiating Increases

Now, the remaining half of the tenants will call, feeling upset. "What do you mean, 50 bucks? That is ridiculous. That's too much; I'm leaving. I can't believe you're doing that to me." So you call back and say, "You are a special and valued tenant. It sounds like $50 is too much for you. We wouldn't do this for everybody but because you called, let's make it $25 for you." "Well, that's better. I sure can't handle $50." It is all marketing.

The technique does work well. Some landlords go further; if they want $25, they ask for $75. Then when people call and say, "I can't handle 75 bucks," they look like a bigger hero by saying, "Well, just for you, it will be $25."

Realize that tenants living in the area will compare notes and find out the rents are different—for similar places. But that's not a problem. Business is business; leases are leases. When you fly on an airplane, you know everyone didn't pay the same amount for the round-trip flight. That's just basic marketing.

Getting rent increases is part of doing business, yet I know so many landlords who haven't asked for a rent increase in eight years. Even if you ask for $20 a month more, it comes to $240 a year; when multiplied by eight, that's almost $2,000 lost. A lot of people work hard for an extra $2,000 a year.

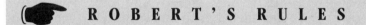

R O B E R T ' S   R U L E S

If you want a $25-a-month rent increase, ask for $50 a month in the letter to the tenants. If they contact you to complain, you can offer them a "compromise" for the $25 you really wanted. Some people might stay and pay the $50; if so, you just got a healthy rent increase.

Sending Out a New Lease

Now, when the lease year is up, do at least two things: (1) remind them about the items in your incentive programs: the ceiling fan, the carpet cleaning, and the brass kickplate; and (2) increase the rent.

I don't care if they have been the best tenants in the world, and you love them like brothers and don't want them to leave—if you don't get a rent increase, you will lose money over time; expenses go up, taxes go up, everything does. Therefore, your rent needs to go up.

When the rent goes up, send out either a new lease, or a lease-update letter, which they sign and return; it then gets attached to the lease as an addendum. We have done both. A lot of times we go back and forth, have them sign a whole new lease or just sign the update: "This updates the lease; the new rent is such and such, and is effective until . . ." There is also nothing wrong with going with two-, three-, and four-year leases, with automatic rent increases. So either way works; each landlord handles the process differently.

You can structure the lease so that it says, "When this lease is up, it continues automatically in force." This includes an automatic rent increase—that is, after 12 months, the $500 rent becomes $550 (or whatever you decide). That protects your interests if you don't sign a new lease.

However, I still prefer them to sign a new lease. They don't need to come into the office; I can send it to them, and they can mail it back in the envelope we include.

Also, I do not recommend that you go on a month-to-month basis with a lease. The only advantage of it is that you can raise the rent every month with 30 days' notice. But I prefer getting a commitment from people, for psychological reasons; we agree up front that the tenants pay for one year or two years. If you go month-to-month, their mind-set is month-to-month, so in three months, they could move out.

I don't want people to move; I want them to stay forever and will do everything I can, within reason, to get them to renew their leases. I prefer if they stay 15 or 20 years—that is how long my mortgages are.

When it comes to raising rents, you have to know your market. For a while in Nashville, rents rose 15 percent and, in some places, even 20 percent. There, rents were going up, while in other markets, they didn't go up at all. It depends on many factors and often doesn't make sense. For example, there are two-bedroom units on my block renting for $350; meanwhile, I am getting $425 and somebody else is renting them for $485.

To set the rents for your properties, I recommend that you look in the Sunday paper at rental ads for places in your neighborhood. Also, call property management companies to compare rents for the kinds of properties you have.

The Cost of Moving

When you notify tenants about rent increases, also send them a letter that explains how expensive it is to move, so they don't react to the rent increase without thinking. (see the sample Tenant Planning to Move Letter in Appendix B). It should say something similar to the following:

> I understand that you're thinking seriously of moving. So I took the liberty of putting together a checklist of the costs you'll have to pay, if you are indeed prepared to move out. I've always felt that I would like to know up front what my entire expenses are going to be before I make a move. So I thought it would be helpful if I included the following checklist I've used in the past so that you don't underestimate the expense of moving. Quite frankly, it can be pretty costly. I've found that out myself the hard way.
>
> Something else: If you do decide to stay, I would certainly appreciate it if you would let us know before I rent the space to someone else. I really would feel terrible if that happened because I've always valued you as a tenant. Anyway, here is the moving checklist that I use—I hope it helps you know in advance the money you will have to come up with:
>
> 1. A security deposit
> 2. Income lost (time off of work)
> 3. First (and possibly the second) month's rent in advance
> 4. The actual moving cost and packing and unpacking costs

5. Deposit on utilities
6. New telephone installation
7. Any items broken and replaced during the move
8. Any other items you may need in the new location

I suggest that you take the same precautions that I do when I move. So my advice is to add up items 1 through 8 to get an idea of the total dollar amount that you'll have to come up with immediately. In any event, I hope this checklist has been helpful. If I can help out in any other way, please let me know.

When we write down how much it will cost them to move—$1,500–$2,000—they think twice about moving. It seems when I move, I never think about it, either. I just go and, suddenly, I have all these bills to pay—truck rental, time lost, and new utilities. So you want to outline what it would cost to move. Then you close the letter with:

"Again, please let me know in the next ten days what you decide, so that I don't lease your unit to someone else without your knowing about it in advance. But you really ought to stay, because otherwise somebody else is going to take it, and we don't want to lose you. It will cost you $1,500 to $2,000 to move now; we hope you decide not to."

This letter works because $1,200 to $2,000 is serious money.

On the other hand, you should also have a letter for tenants you would like to get rid of: "Please get out tomorrow. It is not nearly as expensive as you thought; we will even buy the packing tape and the pickup truck. Besides, we are demolishing that house next Friday . . ."

I suggest you generate these form letters from your computer, have them on file, and send them out as needed. In two minutes, you might have saved yourself $1,000. And that is all there is to it.

CHAPTER 10

Evictions, and How to Avoid Them

Peace is not the absence of conflict. It is the absence of inner conflict.

–Unknown

Let's start by making one thing clear: Even when you have started eviction proceedings, the tenants still live there, unless you stop them. The sheriff is the only official who can move people out of their homes. If you go in for any reason, you could be violating a law, trespassing, and setting yourself up for a lawsuit.

When I go to doctors because I have a health problem, I do what they tell me. Similarly, when I have an eviction, I hand it over to a professional—an eviction/collection attorney. I stop talking to the tenant and do what the eviction attorney tells me to do (or not to do). This protects me because my lawyer takes care of the legalities involved and is covered by malpractice and/or errors-and-omissions insurance. If you handle the process yourself and it is not handled correctly, you risk getting sued. Because laws in every state are different, it's important to involve a local attorney. It also provides me the advantage of separating myself from the relationship with the tenant, so I can say, "We warned you and gave you plenty of chances. Here's the Collection Department. This issue is out of my hands now."

If you want to handle evictions yourself, it's not that complicated, but it requires a lot of steps. According to my experience, if you are willing to deal with tenants, screen them, warn them, and then deal with the problems quickly—not let situations drag on for 30, 40, or 60 days—you can usually avoid evictions. That's clearly a better way to go.

Usually, people involved in eviction cases don't show up in court, so default judgments are common. After the judgment is issued, the tenants have seven to ten days before the sheriff moves them out.

The Eviction Process

In many (but not all) cases, the process includes six steps:

1. The landlord files with the local authorities for an eviction.
2. An eviction notice is served to the tenant by the sheriff's department (sometimes the notice is posted on the door; sometimes it has to be personally handed to the individual).
3. A court date is set (each side has one continuance in which it can reschedule the date).
4. The parties in the dispute show up in court and get a judgment (or a default judgment if one of the parties does not show up).
5. The court gives the delinquent tenant seven to ten days to move out (assuming the judgment is in the landlord's favor).
6. If the tenant does not move out, the landlord files another official paper to get the sheriff to physically get the person out of the property.

The laws regarding this process vary from state to state. For example, in Tennessee, the rent is not late until the fifth day after it is due. In one case, some Vanderbilt University law students who were served with an eviction notice questioned the meaning of the law. As lawyers in training, they loved to be precise with their words and to play with phrases. So they argued, "The rent is due on the 1st. It is not late until the 2nd. Therefore, you cannot say we are late until the 7th. And really it is not late on the 7th until late at night, so it would be the 8th before it would be really late." Realize that there are all kinds of rules about late fees, evictions, and notices. Consult with a local real estate attorney and/or with landlord associations in your area for more information.

Our company policy says the rent is due on the 1st and is late on the 6th. So if payment has not arrived by the 6th, the late fees become part of the amount owed as rent. Some states limit the amount you can charge in late fees; in Tennessee, it is a maximum of 10 percent of the late rent. That means if the rent is $400, we can only charge a $40 late fee on the 6th. If the tenants pay $440 in the next few days, they won't be evicted. But if the 12th comes along and no payment is received, we file for an eviction at the courthouse.

We communicate to tenants by sending a notice that says: "Please pay your rent. You have late fees right now, but if you don't pay the rent, we won't even be able to talk to you about it. You will have to speak with our attorney. Your rent is now $440, but when it goes to the attorney on the 12th, you will have to pay court costs and the attorney's fees. They go up to $550 or more, and you will also be evicted. Please pay your rent; we don't want this to happen to you."

We find they ignore our calls on the 6th, 7th, or 8th, but when they get an eviction notice, it is amazing how quickly they call and attempt to work something out.

Once our attorney files the eviction papers, instead of owing $440, the tenants owe more and we can no longer talk to them directly. They can communicate only with our attorney. If we accept any money from them in the meantime, that stops the eviction process and we have to start over. If they pay money toward what they owe, you have to send them a special receipt that states, "We accept this money, and we are still evicting you [or not evicting you]." If they call and say, "I have the $550 now," you have a decision to make. Can they pay and stay, or are they out? It depends on how you feel about them and the situation.

Collect What Is Owed

Keep in mind that most court judgments stand for between seven and ten years. For example, your tenant John may not have the money to pay the rent today; he may not even have a job. But I bet that over the next seven to ten years, he will get a job or a bank account, and your lawyer will find him and retrieve your money. Before I was married, I let so many people get away with owing rent for a month or two, without following up. Now that I have a wife and a child, I care much more. So I suggest that if you won't collect what is owed for yourself, do it for your family.

Check with your apartment association for recommendations for experienced collection-and-eviction attorneys. Choose one who handles landlord disputes full-time and will skip-trace delinquent tenants every three to six months; some tenants already know the collection attorney well!

Avoiding Eviction

Suppose a tenant fails to pay the rent by the 5th or the 8th of the month, saying, "I can't pay. I don't have a job, and there's all this going on." I suggest you take steps to evict the person, because you need that legal judgment, just in case he or she doesn't move out voluntarily. (And, in the meantime, you can always stop the process if the rent gets paid.) If the tenant doesn't voluntarily move out, you could say, "You know, we could sue you for past rent and keep your deposit, and still come after you later to get all of what you owe. But if you move out by Monday and leave the place looking nice, we will give you $50."

If they leave peacefully, with the place being intact, it would be worth $50 or $100; this is business and every business decision you have to make costs time and money. It's your choice and you can still file an eviction as a backup. But every week you're not collecting rent on your place—and especially if it is a nasty eviction that upsets you and damages your property—it costs you. Remember that with any agreement you make with a tenant, put it in writing, get it signed, and keep a copy.

Evictions also cost you money that you should recover from the tenants. If you don't, you forfeit a lot of money over the next ten years—even tens of thousands of dollars.

Again, a lot of this sounds simple, but most landlords let tenants slide on their rent for three months, then go to Eviction Court. I can assure you that if you don't pay your bank or your credit card company, they will come after you. You should go after the funds you are owed.

R O B E R T ' S   R U L E S

At times, I make agreements and actually pay tenants to leave my units. I figure that paying $100 now is better than paying $900 in damages later; plus, I save months of aggravation and headaches. If you do make such an arrangement, be discreet, so other tenants don't know about it.

What to Do When a Tenant Just Leaves

If you've been evicting a tenant and he just leaves without paying the rent, what do you do? Most landlords would go in, clean up, and start finding new renters. But be careful: The tenant who left still has an interest in that property. In most states, the only person who could evict him or her is the sheriff, who would act through the court. The law doesn't allow you to throw the tenant's belongings out on the street. It is illegal and you could end up with a lawsuit.

If the tenant takes off with his or her possessions but leaves behind a few personal items, the court could say that the tenant hasn't moved. If you throw those things out or start to rerent the place, the tenant could sue and the court could rule that the tenant did not show an intention of leaving (e.g., they found toothbrushes and clothes in the unit). The tenant still lives there; you broke into the apartment, violated the lease, and violated the terms of the eviction. You can get into big trouble, so please be careful.

When it appears a tenant has walked away, we wait to make sure he or she has really left, then we try to make contact. We also take pictures of the condition of the place and all the things in it. Then if the tenant comes back and tries to sue, claiming that thousands of dollars worth of collectible clothes and furniture had been there, we can show the photographs as evidence.

If you do take their possessions out of the unit, you may be obligated to store them for a certain time before you can sell them or give them away. I advise you to know the laws in your area.

Attaching Possessions

Regarding the delinquent tenant's personal belongings, you can state in the lease, and request in the judgment before the court, the possibility of attaching (taking) personal belongings in lieu of rent owed. If you want to do this, you must let the tenants know about that possibility in writing. Attachments could include the TV, household belongings, or even a car. Check with your attorney and find out what the limits are.

Just remember that evictions cost time and create aggravation. In my business, I like to let the professionals do what they do best: I let plumbers do the plumbing, title companies do the title work, and attorneys (who specialize) handle evictions and collections. Because they know the laws—especially new ones, such as the Fair Credit Reporting Act and the Fair Debt Collection Practices Act—it's best to work with them.

Other Ways to "Clean House"

Here are a few tricks some landlords use to avoid eviction. Some are legal, some are not; use your own judgment. For example, one gentleman I know has owned hundreds of properties and never had to evict anybody or go to court. People just pay the rent and move out. You see, he has friendships with members of a motorcycle "gang." (People who belong to motorcycle clubs are often businessmen and businesswomen during the week, and they simply enjoy riding their cycles on the weekend.) For a small fee, this "gang" will drop by his properties on Saturday nights—about 20 of them, on their motorcycles. One of the biggest and meanest-looking cyclists bangs on the door of a delinquent tenant and says, "Hey, you know, Joe, your landlord is a very good friend of ours. He tells us you aren't paying the rent, and we think it is time you should move. Have a nice day." It certainly is amazing how quickly those tenants move out and leave the place in good shape.

Some landlords (who have the utilities of the properties in their names) turn off the electricity if tenants don't pay. In some places this practice is legal; in some, it isn't. It usually works to move people out, but in one situation, it backfired: A tenant called "Caveman" was in violation of his lease; even though we turned off the water and electricity—at that time it was legal—he just kept living there. No matter what we did, he kept living there. He didn't mind, he liked living this way.

Other landlords simply remove the front door, using the excuse that they have to do some repairs. At the same time, they suggest the tenants move out. In most states, this is probably illegal.

Still other landlords cope by deciding to do a lot of work on the property, instead of proceeding with an eviction. They drop in and say, "Hey, I hope you don't mind, but we need to have three or four repairpeople in here to do some maintenance work. They will be drilling." The workers make obnoxious noises and use ill-smelling chemicals to drive the tenants away.

Our society calls this retaliation or harassment. Watch out, because, in most places, it is illegal and tenants can sue you for it.

Most often, all a landlord needs to say is: "The party is over. Time to get out." Realize, though, that if you screen prospective tenants properly, you will avoid many of these problems in the first place (see Chapter 5).

Suing for Possession

Although every court in every state is different, generally you file "Suing for Possession" papers when tenants haven't paid the rent and the judge tells them to move out within ten days. Collection attorneys not only ask for possession, but they also seek monetary judgments. In many cases, you can sue for damages separately, but I still think it is best for a collections attorney to do it up front, get the judgment, and collect on it—if they can be found. They may have to skip-trace them (use information sources to locate people who skip around) to find out, for example, where they work.

Collection attorneys know how to say the right things on the phone, how to get them into court, and so on. In fact, if you followed the correct procedure of having prospective tenants fill out application forms, the information they give helps the collections attorney track them. (See the sample Rental Application in Appendix D.) That's why it's important to include the tenant's Social Security number, name, address, place of employment, and doctor on the form. (When people move around, they generally keep the same doctor; this could be a good clue for the collection attorney who might look for them later.)

Value of Emergency Numbers

In addition to the information stated above, have your tenants provide emergency phone numbers of close relatives. To me, not paying rent, and thus risking eviction, counts as an emergency. I have collected thousands of dollars through emergency numbers. Here's an example: One tenant, Gail, had given her mother's phone number as an emergency contact. I called her mom and said, "Gail, your lovely daughter, has not paid the rent and is about to be evicted." Gail's mother replied, "I am going to go over right now—that good-for-nothing daughter of mine. What does she owe you and where do I pay it?" And the mom paid me the entire $1,800 that Gail owed.

Another time, I called an emergency number when a tenant, Kevin, didn't pay his rent, then got evicted, and had a $2,000 judgment filed against him. I said to Kevin's father, "We have some money for Kevin. Where is he?" We never call to say he owes money; that closes the door. But when we say he gets money, we're told where he lives, where he works, or even where he is right now. Is this legal? As always, check with your local attorney to determine its legality. But it's your money to collect; you should have it.

Document Everything

Once again, remember to document everything you do. We send out a Pay Rent or Quit Letter that says, "Please pay your rent on time. We value you as a tenant. But here is what is going to happen if you don't. You are going to be evicted; you will have to pay court costs; your credit is going to be wrecked; you may never be able to buy a home." (See three sample letters in Appendix B.) Usually, this gets a response; if not, when the eviction has been filed, the phone starts ringing and people show up with money. But by that point, we have to send them over to the attorney.

CHAPTER 11

Letting the Tenant Rent-to-Own

The function of freedom is to free somebody else.

—Toni Morrison

One of the most useful and mutually beneficial ways of being creative in the landlord/tenant relationship is the rent-to-own, or lease-option, approach. This has the double advantage of creating an extra (and nonrefundable) cash flow for the landlord, while offering tenants a way to build equity and eventually purchase their own property.

"Rent-to-own" means the tenant rents your property with an option to buy it. This eventually takes the property out of your hands and, if all goes according to plan, you will no longer be its owner, let alone its landlord. However, even though this is a book about landlording, I do want to mention this alternative, because it can really cut down on your rental headaches. (See Appendix A for more information.)

Saying this may upset many landlords, but I think you are always better off doing rent-to-own/lease-option with houses and duplexes than you are by renting them. You may protest because if tenants buy your home, you have to give up your rental property. But the profits are really on your side. Here's an example: You buy a house for

$50,000; you lease-option it for $72,000 over time; you've made $22,000 by the time you sell it. It's okay that you might have to pay some taxes on the sale; if you are a serious real estate investor, you simply buy another house.

Option Money versus the Security Deposit

Now, if you just rent a property to someone, you would ask one month's rent as a security deposit—$500 or $600, for example. This money has to go into a special bank account; it is not yours and you risk getting sued if you don't treat it right. When your tenants move out and leave the place in decent shape, you are obligated to give their deposit back to them. If you don't, you have to write them a letter that itemizes all of your reasons for keeping their deposit. This process needs to be handled fairly or you are violating the law. But with a lease-option situation, that money is yours.

Remember my suggestion about how to set rents? You ask prospective tenants how much they are looking to spend and work out an agreement. So do the same with lease-options. Ask how much they are willing to put toward a down payment on the house. If they offer $1,500, then work with them. If they offer only $200, you probably wouldn't rent to them anyway (unless it's a low-end property for which that rent is common).

Over time, I have asked a lot of people, "How much are you willing to put toward a down payment for a rent-to-own property?" Although some have given me unbelievably low figures, I have also received answers like $6,000 for a $60,000 house. In one case, four months after the lease-optioners paid $6,000 in option money, the people moved to Texas and we kept their option money. Some prefer to spend an extra $300 in rent each month to build up their option money account—that adds up to $3,600 a year. By comparison, if we rented that same place and accepted a security deposit, we certainly wouldn't be making a profit.

ROBERT'S RULES

In Chapter 3, I suggested letting the marketplace set your rent prices for you. You ask the magic question, "What are you looking to spend?" The same principle holds true for lease-option situations. Ask, "How much are you willing to put toward a down payment on the house?" If they say an amount higher than what you expected, you'll have more money to work with.

An advantage of option money is that you will not be taxed on it until the option gets exercised (i.e., when the lease-optioner leaves or the sale closes). Let's say Joe is a tenant with a three-year option to buy one of my houses for $72,000. He gives me $2,000 in option money and I put it in the bank. Three years later, Joe takes off. I am now taxed on that option money because Joe has turned down the option by leaving. That result is a much better one than a security deposit, which you have to give back when tenants move out. With security deposits, if tenants don't pay rent on time, they lose their deposits and consequently, their credit is affected. With lease-options, if tenants pay the rent late, they forfeit their option money. That provision is written into the lease-option agreement. The advantage is that it becomes a serious incentive to pay rent; people don't want to lose their option money.

In some cases, it makes sense to charge a security deposit in addition to the option money. However, if the tenants give me a sizable amount, I don't require it. The option money becomes my security against expenses for any future damages or against skipped rent payments.

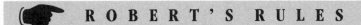

Don't make the Option to Purchase Agreement part of the lease. Indeed, when you set up a rent-to-own arrangement, you want to have two separate documents, a lease and an option agreement. (Sometimes I use a Contract for Sale, with a Contingency Clause; that is the same as an option.) I separate them because if tenants don't pay and I have to take them to court, I don't want to confuse the judge with one document that includes items like lease-option, a rent-to-own agreement, and a Contract for Sale. It would add unnecessary complications.

Lease-Options—The Best Choice Available

I offer lease-option to almost all of my tenants because I believe everyone is better off doing rent-to-own/lease-options than renting. I prefer that my tenants buy a property and become homeowners; then I can buy more properties. I am providing a service and making money in the process. And I frequently don't even have to give up the house. Statistically, only one out of four or five tenants who sign rent-to-own agreements follow through on them.

Let's say I have a rental house worth $50,000, and I lease-option it for $60,000 or $65,000 as the sale price, taking appreciation into account. I have to stay within a reasonable price; I cannot sell a $50,000 house for $90,000, but I can work with a 20 percent leeway. (Appraising houses isn't an exact science—two appraisers can be apart in their numbers by as much as 20 percent. My goal is to get top dollar for a selling price—maybe even 5 percent above top dollar.)

Tenants don't care about the total property price as much as they do about the rent they have to pay each month and the amount of the down payment. In my experience, 97 percent of renters want to become homeowners, but they face obstacles: They just don't have the necessary down payment or credit, or they don't know how to go about buying a house. That makes lease-option a valuable service.

After a year of renting, people can often find financing for a mortgage in order to pay me off. It's a mutually beneficial way to do business. My company is affiliated with a mortgage company called United Funding Group, which has all kinds of mortgages for renters, lease-optioners, and investors. We send an application form to a prospective tenant who wants a lease-option, and the mortgage representative lets us know if the person can qualify for a loan. Then we work out a down payment and a payment schedule. Usually with a rent-to-own agreement, lease-optioners are able to buy their homes within a year—and we can turn over a lot of houses this way.

Rental Rates on an Option

If I set the rent for a house at $500 a month, can I charge more rent—say, $600—for the tenant's right to buy this house? Yes, I would apply that additional $100 to the tenant's purchase price and have an extra $1,200 a year. This definitely provides incentive for renters to pay on time and stick around. And if they don't live up to their commitments, I still have $1,200 in the bank.

Be sure to separate these figures in the paperwork. Mortgage companies need to see what has been paid into the lease-option agreement on top of the rent, so be sure to break them out on the documents. (See the sample Option to Purchase Real Estate form in Appendix C.)

The Pride of Ownership

Another advantage of lease-option is not having to deal with repairs. It's called the "pride of ownership." With a lease-option, I say, "Congratulations. This is your home now and you get to fix it. Don't call me unless the roof caves in or something happens that's covered by insurance."

Rent readiness is not as critical, either. When I advertise a property as a "Handyman Special, Rent-to-Own, Own Your Own Home, Last Chance Home Ownership Program," tenants are inclined to paint and clean it themselves. They put up with less perfection in the beginning, and that saves me time and money.

I certainly screen lease-optioners, too. If their references check out, I might say, "Instead of paying me $2,000 in initial option money, you only have to pay $1,000, but you do all the work on the place. Is that a good deal?" If they agree, I save money when getting the place ready. As I noted here, people really want to own their own homes. What's more, they take better care of it over time. They have the pride of ownership.

Handyman Specials

A few years ago, I got a great deal when I bought eight houses in run-down, almost condemnable condition. I even thought about bulldozing them. Then my phone started ringing: "Do you own that house on Lillian Street?" I said yes. A caller said, "I want to rent it." I was stunned. I said, "You've got to be kidding; these houses are dumps." The caller said, "I still want one of those houses." Actually, about ten people called me; it became a lesson in knowing my market.

One of the callers said, "I'm a carpenter, my wife's an electrician, my cousin's a plumber. We'll fix up the house." His whole family worked "in the trade." So I offered him a lease-option. I actually felt so badly about the condition of the place that I gave him $300 to buy some basics. Still, the place needed a lot of work just to get it up to the standards of the building codes.

So he moved in, fixed up the whole place, paid rent for three years (I gave him a break on the rent for all the work he did), and then left. I still owned a nice house and kept the option money. If I had done all the work on the place, I would have spent thousands of dollars just to get it up to code standards. I could have rented it but would probably have never recouped the money I would have put into repairs. What a bonus I got!

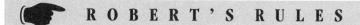

ROBERT'S RULES

Some investors make a lot of money with lease-options. I know a young woman in Ohio who has purchased 110 run-down homes. She simply buys these houses; she doesn't touch them. Instead, she runs an ad that says, "Handyman Special . . . Rent-to-Own . . . Become a Homeowner . . . You Fix It . . . You Clean It Up." She is not in the maintenance business, nor is she in the repair business, nor the painting business—and she makes a fortune. She knows her market.

Other Factors to Consider

Lease-optioners are responsible for repairs, but that can also be the downside of this deal. The pride of ownership should make a difference, but it doesn't in all cases. I recommend that you still regularly inspect the houses and set up specific timetables you both agree on for repairs. If your lease-optioner doesn't fix the leaky sink for six months, you could have a $4,000 floor problem. And that could be just the tip of the iceberg. So make a point of periodically inspecting every property you have a financial interest in.

When people rent-to-own, they have a lease-option that says, "If you don't pay the rent on time, the option is gone. If you don't do the repairs like you say you will, the option is also gone . . . ." In addition, I have the lease-optioners write this statement: "I promise to pay the rent on time. If I don't, I lose my option to buy. I will make the repairs we have talked about. If I don't within X amount of time, I lose my option. I understand that in one year, my option will expire. If I don't get a new loan and close you out, I will lose my option. Or, in one year, I can renew my option for a $500 fee; plus, my payment will go up and the price will go up. "

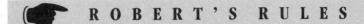

ROBERT'S RULES

When the lease-optioner signs a Lease Option Agreement, have the person also write, in their own handwriting, a statement that shows he or she understands that agreement. For example, it would say, "I promise to pay the rent on time. If I don't, I lose my option. I will make the repairs we have talked about. If I don't within X amount of time, I lose my option. I understand that in one year, my option will expire. If I don't get a new loan and close out the sale, I will lose it."

Get Investors Started with Lease-Options

With lease-options, I can approach other investors and give them a chance to get started in the rental property business. People want to invest in real estate but often don't have enough money for down payments or enough credit to borrow for a mortgage. So I say, "Give me some money down as option money, a few thousand dollars. The gross rent on my duplex is $900 a month, $450 per side. The cost of my note is $400 a month. So you pay me $600 a month, rent it out, and keep the extra $300. You'll build some equity as the property appreciates." If you set up your agreements effectively, lease-optioning can work in a mutually beneficial way.

Lending a Helping Hand

Lease-optioners care more about home ownership than about price. They care about getting into a home with no money down and will take out a second mortgage to help themselves out. They're often unclear about the actual purchase prices. So we like to be up front and write out the agreement as well as what their monthly payment would be.

Yet if they pay regularly for one year, their credit can go almost to a perfect credit rating unless they have bankruptcies or other bad credit on their record. But it's possible to see credit go from a C or a D to a B or an A in a year. Then they can apply to one of the phenomenal loan programs available.

So here's a question to consider: Will you accept a second mortgage when your tenant/owner pays responsibly and takes care of the place but just doesn't have the credit to handle it alone? I have done it, because it's all a matter of numbers and money. But the answer is: It depends. Instead of explaining the concept here, I suggest you discuss it with your lenders and your accountants to see if this approach makes sense for you.

Lease-Option Summary

The advantages of lease-optioning far outweigh the disadvantages:

- You get cash on the sale and walk away with a profit.
- You provide a way for people to own their own homes when their credit is poor.
- You get out of the repair business.
- People are more likely to pay rent faithfully because they don't want to forfeit their option money.
- If you have difficulty collecting rent, you can keep the option money instead of going through the eviction process.

The disadvantages include the following:

- You have to pay taxes on your profits (but that shows prosperity).
- You have to keep up with inspections and repairs.
- You have to enforce your policies and procedures to make it all work.

Some landlords consider giving up the home a disadvantage because the rental property gets sold over time; others see that as an advantage. Overall, I believe this is the best option for serious landlords who want to have a profitable business and help others have a home of their own.

CHAPTER 12

Protecting Your Interests with Insurance

I have been through some terrible things in my life, some of which actually happened.

–Mark Twain

People often ask what kind of insurance they need as a landlord. I emphasize the absolute importance of getting the following:

- Title insurance. Some landlords protest that they don't want to spend $300 to buy title insurance on $20,000 properties. But they throw their money away if the seller doesn't legally own the properties they want to buy. It's essential to make sure who owns the title.
- Fire/liability insurance. I have become a reluctant expert on this because (1) I do believe in protecting my assets, and (2) I recently had 28 properties damaged by tornadoes. Don't cut corners. In fact, you should always insure your property for top value. It's dangerous to say, "I bought it for $40,000, it's worth $80,000; I'll insure it for $60,000. If you don't insure your property for top value, and it gets destroyed, the insurance company will discount what they give you.

☞ **R O B E R T ' S   R U L E S**

Always include a Replacement Rider on your policy so that the insurance company will replace the full value of your property even if its value goes up or the cost of wood triples next year. Without that much insurance, you will likely receive less than the property is worth. This is true even for partial destruction. Let's say you lost the kitchen to flood damage and it is worth $10,000. If you were underinsured, the insurance payment may turn out to be $6,000, or whatever percentage of the whole amount is covered. This is your hedge against inflation.

Your policy will have a liability section, so always read the exceptions for items not covered. (For example, employee injuries are not covered—see the discussion on workers' compensation in this chapter.) Here's an example. A contractor/landlord hired someone to go work on a deck at one of his properties. He spent his time hauling wood and helping the contractor. They built it big enough to comfortably hold 12 people.

Then he sold the house, and the new owner held a big party for about 29 people on the deck. It broke, injuring several people who had to go to the hospital. So a lawyer contacted about 18 injured people who were on this deck and instituted a lawsuit. They sued the contractor for a couple of million dollars. They also sued the previous owner of the property, who also happened to be the guy who had worked on the deck. So the previous owner called his insurance company. The agent told him his property was insured, that he was covered for property liability if someone tripped, or if there were a fire, or if someone were killed. But because he was also the contractor, he needed contractor's insurance. He wasn't covered. Though he countersued and won some concessions, he mostly had to cover the entire lawsuit on his own.

You have to know whether activities you are doing are covered by your insurance policies. If you are building, rehabbing, or painting, get a contractor's or a builder's insurance policy.

Management Insurance

The property liability in landlord insurance will cover a lot, if a tenant gets hurt, for example. But if you manage your own properties, consider management insurance. This is why it is good to hire a management company with its own management insurance. If that company upsets the tenant, they get sued, instead of you. I have a management company called Superior Properties and I have incorporated it. It handles management of my properties and collects the rents. It has its own liability insurance, so if I get sued, I am covered through both property insurance and management insurance.

Umbrella Policy

Another good insurance value is having an umbrella policy, which covers a variety of insurance needs. Call your insurance agent and say, "Hey, I want an umbrella policy." I estimate you can get a million-dollar umbrella for a few hundred dollars a year. I think this is one of the best deals going. Ask your insurance agent about full details on a comprehensive umbrella policy.

Workers' Compensation Insurance

Even if you do have contractors working for you, rather than actual employees, I suggest you take out a workers' compensation (workers' comp) policy.

For example, if you pay people an hourly wage to do property maintenance on a regular basis, they are probably considered employees. So if an accident happens, you may be liable for covering them as employees. You can sign a waiver if you have fewer than three employees (the number can differ from state to state). But with more employ-

---

☞ R O B E R T ' S   R U L E S

My best advice is to get clear about exactly what activities you're doing, and to then contact your insurance agent and ask what kind of coverage you really need. You want to be well insured for all possible business scenarios you may encounter.

---

ees than three, state laws require you to have workers' comp insurance. I recommend you buy the coverage even if it's not required by law. If your maintenance man, who works 20 hours a week for you, falls off the roof and gets hurt, you should be covered—for no other reason than that the injured worker might be enticed to call a lawyer advertised on TV, and to try to take you to court for damages.

Weird cases have had their day in court. Here's one. A landlord hires a man named John to cut the grass. John is a subcontractor responsible for the repairs and maintenance on the equipment he uses, and for his own insurance and licenses; John is clearly not an employee. John goes out and hires Bubba to do yard work by the hour. While Bubba is cutting the grass, he accidentally cuts his foot off. Who's responsible for Bubba's medical bills? The court says, "Well, John wasn't an employee, because he signed all the waivers, and they didn't have an employee relationship." But Bubba actually is an employee. John should have had worker's comp but he didn't. Because of all of the agency subcontractor provisions, the homeowner is the employer, so he's obligated to actually pay the amount the foot is worth. (It sounds disgusting, but insurance people use a book that spells out what a finger is worth, a foot, a back, or a neck.) Because a foot is said to be worth $28,000, that is what the homeowner has to pay.

As a landlord, the best thing for you to do is to say, "John, I work with you a lot and would like to continue our relationship, and want to make a long-term arrangement. So I will give you all my business, but I require you to get workers' comp. Even if you have to charge more to cover the costs, let's work it out here. If you are on my properties all the time, you need to get workers' comp."

If John or the homeowner had had workers' compensation, the issue would have been clear-cut. This lesson indicates the importance of checking in with your insurance agent and saying, "I don't think I have any employees. I don't have any payroll. But I want a minimum policy that will cover me for workers' comp."

My company pays about $700 a year in insurance to cover our employees (as defined by workers' comp). Now if Sammy does a small job every six months, I probably don't need the coverage. But if he comes every week and works mainly for me and I pay him by the hour, the courts will probably consider Sammy to be my employee. I just want to let you know: Be careful. Call your insurance agents and ask for their advice.

Meanwhile, whatever understanding you may have with your insurance agent about getting insurance, document it—just as you do in every other part of your business. If you do get sued, you have evidence in your files and you can sue your insurance agent if necessary.

Other Insurance Issues

When 28 of my properties got hit by a tornado, I had the most complete insurance coverage possible—and yet the insurance company wouldn't pay me. This incident almost put me out of business.

Initially, they promised to cover needed repairs after a tornado had hit my properties. I said, "I will have to write a lot of checks for people to get repairs done. Will you pay me?" I was told: "Robert, we will get you the check tomorrow. Just bring us an invoice and we will have your check."

I had to spend $10,000 in about eight days. And when I submitted an invoice, they wouldn't write me the check—so much for my great insurance policy. This went on and on; then they offered much less than the actual repair costs. I hired a law firm and the lawyers succeeded in getting my claim after quadrupling the amount of my invoice. This convinced me I needed an ongoing relationship with a lawyer.

Need for Legal Insurance

I have been sued several times as a landlord. Most of the suits concerned trivial eviction processes, but one actually amounted to $28,000. When one of my tenants abandoned his apartment but left all of his furnishings in it, we called him. He told us to throw his possessions away. Instead, we stored them for 30 days. Finally, we threw them out. Then the ex-tenant hired a lawyer and claimed we had thrown out $28,000 worth of his property. Fortunately, I had a prepaid legal insurance policy (which is explained later in this chapter). So I went to my attorney, who called the ex-tenant's attorney and said, using some intimidation, "I represent the firm of Blackburn, Slocum, Freeman & Haffner in Nashville, Tennessee. Do you know who we are?" He certainly did because this is one of the top law firms in the state. My lawyer continued, "You know Robert Shemin of Shemin Superior Properties?" He said, "Well, yes, we are suing Mr. Shemin." My lawyer said: "Well, Robert has us on retainer, and we represent him in this firm and you have sued him. Now we are going to go to court and defend Robert, because we think he is innocent. If we lose, we are going to appeal. If you don't drop the suit, we are going to countersue. We are a big firm with 30 attorneys and we are coming after you." They dropped the suit in a few minutes. In my earlier years, I would have hired some unknown attorney for $500 and spent a lot of time and money in court.

Here are examples of why I would call: "My tenant is threatening to sue me; my car repair guy won't fix something; I have a complicated insurance legality problem; I am looking at this deal and facing some legal issues, I need to understand a tax law question; I want you to write a letter about a dispute, make a call to a contractor who isn't being fair. I want to call you at any time and I expect you to give me answers. I want you to be willing to say, 'You had better make it right with Robert. I represent a very big law firm, so fix it or we are going to court.'"

I also sign a lot of contracts and documents, which I don't always read carefully (who does?). When a disagreement occurs a year down the road, I realize I shouldn't have signed that document. "I want you as my attorney to look at this contract before I sign it. What would this service cost?"

Your Own Will

Consider this: 70 percent of Americans do not have a will. Everybody needs a will unless they have nothing and don't care about anyone else. I need a comprehensive will—not a fill-in-the-blanks one, but a big-time will that often gets reviewed and changed. So I say, "Assets change, relationships change, so a will has to change and I want it done right. And so I want you as my lawyer to also review my will every year."

Several months ago, I talked with some really good friends—a couple with two young children—about getting their will written. Three months later, they were both killed in a car accident. Luckily, the kids weren't with them. But because both parents died without a will, the state took control of their kids. Despite the fact that two sets of grandparents would have cared for them, the state put them in foster care after a wait of 90 days. The state also froze all the family assets, including bank accounts, because that's what happens when there's no will. When it all clears up, the children will probably lose about a third of the estate, which they should have been entitled to.

Pre-Paid Legal Services

Lawyers might want to charge me a lot for all the services I need, but I already have an excellent insurance solution—a pre-paid legal service from a company that charges $25 a month (in most states). Called

Pre-Paid Legal Services, it is a national, publicly traded company that has been in business for 25 years.

Pre-Paid Legal Services covers these six areas:

1. Any legal need that you have, or anyone in your family has, is covered. This includes you, your spouse, and your children, through college age. Disabled children are covered for life.

2. If you get a traffic ticket anywhere in the United States, the service sends a good lawyer to court on your behalf. When I got a ticket in Alabama, a lawyer represented me in court and got the judgment thrown out. Not only did it save me court costs and a ticket fee, but it also saved money on car insurance.

3. If you get into a car wreck and someone dies, you could be charged with vehicular homicide/manslaughter, whether you are guilty or innocent. Your car insurance doesn't cover that; it only pays for medical bills and car accidents. But if you have pre-paid legal coverage, a law firm will represent you with no limits.

4. While a REALTOR® was driving down the road talking on her cell phone, she hit another car head-on. Someone in the other car died and she was charged with manslaughter. For her $25 a month, her lawyers went to court and she was found not guilty. That legal bill would otherwise have been about $15,000.

5. With Pre-Paid Legal Services, if your tenants or anyone else names you in a civil lawsuit, you have 75 hours of an attorney's time. If you don't use that time right away, it accumulates. I guarantee this will take care of any nuisance lawsuits, and most real ones.

6. If you are audited by the IRS for this year's or last year's tax return, this service will pay for 50 hours of a tax attorney's time. (Why does the IRS audit people like you and me? They get money. They don't audit big corporations because they have armies of accountants and lawyers to defend themselves, but we don't.)

This service does not cover criminal cases; it is related to civil cases or work-related criminal ones. If you got charged, for example, with sexual harassment or malfeasance at work, or something similar, your attorney's fees would be covered under work-related criminal or civil suits.

If you sign up with Pre-Paid Legal Services, you get 50 hours of a tax attorney's time if you are named in an audit, and that makes a big difference. You won't talk just to a regular attorney, but to one who specializes in tax law. Wherever you are located, in whatever city, county, or state, they will get a referral lawyer to help you—all this for $25 a month.

Along with all the other services, anything that is not covered—and there are some things that are not covered: a bankruptcy filing, divorce filings, and some more complicated procedures—you get an unlimited number of phone consultations, as well as a true 25 percent discount for uncovered services. So instead of paying $160 an hour, for example, you pay around $95 a hour.

Service issues are important—if I have only one attorney and my phone calls are never returned, I have little recourse. I could call the local bar association and file a complaint, but resolution takes months. Instead, Pre-Paid Legal Services provides an open-ended contract at $25 a month, which is tax-deductible at the end of the year. There is a one-time $10 signup fee and no other requirements. They provide phone consultations; they will write letters and make phone calls, review contracts, and do a comprehensive, fully documented will (normally costing $600-$700). If you want to meet with attorneys, you can. The service guarantees a 24-hour (business-day) response time. If you are not happy with your assigned attorney, you can call an 800 number and customer service will make sure an attorney takes care of you. They also guarantee a 48-hour response time.

Legal Insurance Summary

- If you get a traffic or a speeding ticket anywhere in the United States, or if you have any kind of legal question, Pre-Paid Legal Services will take care of it nationally.

- If you have a question about a specific state law, the company has firms everywhere.
- If you are named in a lawsuit, they will give you 75 hours of an attorney's time.
- If you don't use their services right away, you can accumulate your time.
- The service becomes effective immediately. If you sign up—on the Internet, over the phone, or by fax—and then run somebody over and get sued, they will defend you.
- If you get audited by the IRS, legal services are covered.
- You sign an open-ended contract that you can cancel at any time.

 ROBERT'S RULES

I recommend that you sign up for this service if only to take care of the writing of your will. For an application fee of $10 and $25 for the first month, get your will done and have a chance to find out more about their services. You can cancel Pre-Paid Legal Services at any time. I have used this service for some of the most complicated real estate questions, and found that they only work with top-notch attorneys. I think everybody in real estate—or those in any business for themselves—should consider this plan. I highly recommend that you take a look at it.

(The Pre-Paid Legal Services plans differ in many states and are subject to certain restrictions, which are explained in their literature. If you are interested in more information, please visit my Web site at <www.shemin.com> or call my office at 888-302-8018.)

Property Acquisition And Financing

Secrets of a Millionaire Landlord is not about how to find, and pay for, property to rent. However, here is a brief overview, with some tips, on both areas, as well as more information on lease-optioning.

How to Find Good Deals

If you don't have a house, you have nothing to rent, so you are not going to be a landlord. There must be at least 37 different ways to find good deals. Most people pick a couple of methods, learn them well, and stick to them. Let me tell you four of my best sources for finding good deals: bad landlords, finance companies, foreclosures, and driving around.

Bad Landlords and Management Companies

My number-one method has been locating bad landlords and management companies. From a business viewpoint, most landlords don't really know what they are doing.

That is a generalization, and I hate to make it, but I think it is absolutely true. A bad landlord, in almost every case, bought a piece of property that was expected to bring in serious cash flow automatically. Then the tenant (who has never been screened) damages something and doesn't pay rent. The landlord pulls the tenant into Eviction Court and it's a hassle. And that landlord becomes a highly motivated seller. Further, after the hurricane season, it's common to find motivated sellers in parts of Florida.

Among bad landlords who are motivated to sell, they often own more than one property, so investors like me buy a group of properties at one time. I keep my ears open for news about unhappy landlords.

I have also found good deals on property through management companies. If a bad management company manages hundreds of units, there could be a lot of disgruntled landlords that are saying, "This property has not brought in a cash flow in two years; I am losing money. Take it! Get it off my hands!" This is all because the company never screened prospective tenants, didn't do repairs, and didn't know how to save money. What started as a great deal became a bad investment due to mismanagement.

Finance Companies

Another good source for finding deals is found among finance companies—higher-risk lending institutions like the Associates, Beneficial, and mortgage companies that make high-risk loans. (These differ from the big banks and big mortgage companies, which make loans to people with A+ credit, so they don't have a high foreclosure rate.) These companies make the 10- to 15-percent-interest loans, with an 80-percent loan-to-value risk, and work with people whose credit is shaky. These finance companies are listed in the Yellow Pages. If you call them every two months, eventually, you will probably find a deal. Because of their high-risk nature, opportunities come along a lot more often than with banks.

Foreclosures

Foreclosures are also a good source of deals. In some years, 1 out of 70 homes in the United States goes into foreclosure. That's about 1.4 million foreclosures that are on the market in a year. As the economy turns downward, the numbers will increase.

I like to purchase these from the finance company after the foreclosure paperwork has been completed, although sometimes I run an ad in the paper before a family foreclosure. The ads says, "Are you in trouble? Can I help you with your note?" That way, I can often find a deal before the place has lost some of its value through neglect.

In today's world, a lot of property is overleveraged and this can pose problems. If a house is worth $60,000 and someone has a $64,000 loan against it, there's no room to maneuver. Foreclosures can therefore be an excellent source.

Driving Around

Simply driving around, looking for For Rent and For Sale signs, and getting the word out helps me get good deals. Pick an area you like, and drive around looking for vacant homes. If a property has been for rent for a long time, that might mean the landlord is highly motivated to sell. This is true for apartments, too.

Bear in mind that most good deals require a lot of repair work. If a house is beautifully fixed up with new carpets, the owner won't let it go for below-market value. The best deal I ever got involved in was my own home. Listed by the biggest real estate company in town, and located in one of the most desirable neighborhoods, it had three feet of garbage on the floor and stuff falling from the ceiling. I couldn't even get into the basement, because garbage was blocking the entrance. Others said it would cost a lot to fix it. I bought it for $40,000. I knew instantly I could rehab it for a lot less, and did so. Most people don't want to do the repair work, but we make our money by "messing" with places nobody wants to deal with.

Buying the Property

Let's face it: Real estate is not real estate; it is finance. You can take an average deal and, with great financing, turn it into a great deal. Profit-making rental companies understand how to buy houses by using other people's money, and by using credit. They're really in the finance business.

People commonly think that, to be a landlord, you need to get a big pile of money, buy a house for $80,000, and take time to recoup the investment. Or they believe you need to borrow $80,000 and have perfect credit to buy property. But in three years, I have bought hundreds of houses without using my own money. Now I sometimes use a credit line. But at first, I didn't have the credit to get a credit line. Instead, I went to private investors and paid higher interest rates for the money until I established a credit line.

Then I bought the property for cash, so I bought it quickly and got a better deal. That beats most buyers, who spend 90 days looking around for financing before they can close a deal. Within 20 to 60 days, I refinance the property I just bought. The mortgage companies are making 70-percent loan-to-value deals on properties right now; so are banks. Mortgage companies may even let you buy single-family homes or duplexes with only 10 percent down if you have good credit and provide credit to do repairs. That way, I'm not tying up my own money. Added to that, an appraiser can say a home will require $20,000 in repairs, whereas I can get them done for $10,000. The difference becomes the down payment.

There are other ways of creatively financing a deal. For example, if you lease the property for a month, the mortgage company will call it a refinance deal and you can renegotiate with better terms. Find a good mortgage company and/or bank to work with, and get creative with how you finance the deals.

Shopping for Interest Rates

Although some people make a big thing about interest rates, I don't really care. If the deal is a good one, I will do it even if I don't get the lowest interest rate. I always look at cash–cash, money–money. I would rather borrow money at 8 percent, but if I'm paying 9 or 10 percent, instead of a lower rate, and the deal still works, it doesn't matter. I would rather take a thousand deals at 10 percent than two at 7 percent if, in the long run, I am buying them and riding the cash flow.

Lenders are in a highly competitive situation, so I recommend shopping around. Check two, three, or even four sources for each deal. Make the lenders aware of the lowest rate and the best terms you have received so far, and give each one the chance to match or beat it. Keep negotiating.

Also, beware of accepting any loan with a balloon or a call payment that becomes due in one, three, or five years down the road. The biggest expense in owning or managing a property is the cost of capital on your money. Once that expense is set, it is set. You can save $1,000 or even $10,000 a year by getting a better interest rate. That is money saved and locked in for a long time. Take your time and negotiate, negotiate, negotiate—it is well worth it.

Lease-Optioning—The "Other" Realty Investment Option

Here's one example of how lease-optioning works: I will lease-option Joe's house for $350 a month at an option price of $40,000, and then I will turn around to Mary and say, "Hey, here is your big chance to own a home. You can lease-option it from me at a rent of $500 a month and buy it for $48,000." I don't own it; I don't even have a note; I don't have a lot of liability or responsibility, yet I have two leases and two options. And if I am smart enough (and I'm screening lease-optioners effectively enough), she gets a mortgage and closes on the purchase, and I walk away with $15,000–$18,000. I haven't tied up my credit, or borrowed money, or taken a lot of money out of the bank, but I've made money.

As a matter of fact, I may even get up-front money because Joe is a disgruntled landlord, so I may not have to give him up-front money; I can negotiate with Joe because the place needs painting and repairs. So now, I receive $1,500 in up-front option money from Mary, so I put that in my pocket, and get $200 a month coming in. My role is to make sure Mary pays me so that I can pay Joe the rent.

This approach works on high-end properties as well as low-end ones. There are a lot of people who go to builders and REALTORS® about houses that won't sell in the $100,000 to $400,000 range. Or, maybe the contractor's note is $1,800 a month. I pay the contractor $1,800 and find someone who will rent-to-own it for $2,700. On a house like that, I get some option money up front: $5,000, maybe even $15,000.

People who have attended my real estate course and learned about lease-optioning have acquired 20 or 30 high-end homes and average a cash flow of between $500 and $800 a month on each house. One couple is earning $20,000 to $30,000 a month in profit, just on lease-optioning. It's a mutually beneficial situation and it's a wonderful way to have more freedom. My real estate classes can get you started. For more information, go to my Web site at <www.shemin.com>.

Quick Landlording Forms

The following are forms that I use in my business. Several of the forms have been used with permission from <www.mrlandlord.com> (Web site for landlords). Please feel free to adapt them.

However, be aware that every state has different laws regarding property ownership and renting. You will want to have your attorney review these laws before you use them.

Special Thank-You Letter to Tenants Moving In
Welcome Letter to Tenants
Move-In Payment Schedule
Move-In Inspection Report
Monthly Inspection Report for Month of _____
Happy Holidays!
Maintenance Guarantee
Preparation Checklist for Colder Weather
Rental Upkeep Violation Notice
Letter Sent to Tenants When Trash Is a Problem
Garbage Violation Notice
Personal Letter to a Problem Tenant
Returned Check Notice
Partial Payment Acceptance Notice

Pay Rent or Quit Letter
30 Days' Notice to Terminate Tenancy
Form Indicating Grounds for Eviction
Tenant Planning to Move Letter
Vacancy Makeover Checklist
Return of Security Deposit upon Move-Out

SPECIAL THANK-YOU LETTER TO TENANTS MOVING IN

What you're after in this letter is to begin the process of forging a happy and responsible tenant relationship. You also want to show that you're a caring person and that you're delighted to have them as tenants. This letter begins to set up a warm, caring, me-to-you tone.

Dear _____,

I want to write to you, at this special time when you're moving in, to tell you how grateful I am to have you as a tenant. In the years that I have owned this property, no one has ever had more loyal and more dedicated tenants than I have. And it is people like yourself who deserve a good share of the credit for making this possible. I'm sure that, over the years, I will hold your support and your friendship as a very special blessing.

Sincerely,

Your Name

WELCOME LETTER TO TENANTS

This is an example of a recognition and acknowledgment letter that begins to establish a warm and caring long-term relationship with a tenant.

Dear _____,

One of my favorite duties, which I really enjoy, is the privilege of welcoming new tenants to our neighborhood. I just want you to know that we are dedicated to serving your needs. And our intent is to do it efficiently, courteously, and promptly. So if there are any questions you may have concerning your dwelling or the neighborhood in general, please give me a call and I or my staff will assist you. Or if at any time in the future there is a matter that may arise because of a change of any kind, please let us know.

I've been asked to remind you of the following:

The rent is always due at _____ and no later than the _____ of every month.

If you are paying by check, we ask that you please make the check payable to _____ and mail it to _____.

And, if you do find that you need any repairs, please call:

Sincerely,

Your name

P.S. Please accept this note as a cordial greeting to you personally.

WELCOME LETTER TO TENANTS (Option 2)

Dear _____,

We would like to welcome you to your new home. We hope that you will be very happy here and we will try our best to make sure you're satisfied.

We wanted to let you know a couple of things about your new home:

1. If you need a repair, please call our office at _____. If we are not in the office, please leave a detailed message on our service, including your name, phone number, address, and information about the problem you are having. Our office will get back in touch with you as soon as possible and our service-person will be out to fix the problem. When the repair has been made, please call our office and let us know.

2. We guarantee all repairs will be completed within three days from the time you call. Most repairs will be completed within 24 hours.

3. If you want to plant trees or bushes outside the house, we will reimburse you for half the cost, up to $ _____, if you plant them and promise to take care of them. Remember that the trees and bushes stay with the property should you move.

4. In order to make sure your rent is never late, your rental payment of $ _____ must be mailed no later than the _____ day of the month and should be sent to: _____.

5. We want your stay with us to be a happy one and we will work with you to make sure you are always satisfied. All we ask of you is to pay your rent on time and keep your home nice and neat. We have a strict policy of collecting late fees and evicting

if your rent is not paid on time. Late fees accrue if your rent payment is not received by the _____ day of the month. In addition, if your rent payments are not received by the _____ day of the month, our attorneys will seek collection and eviction and will report the unpaid rent to both credit reporting agencies and the IRS. We hope this never happens, so please pay your rent on time.

6. If you would like to renew your lease with us, we will install, as a gift to you, a _____ and/or _____ (a value of over $40). Remember that these gifts are for your enjoyment while you stay with us. But if you leave, these gifts stay with the property.

Again, we hope you are happy with your new home, and if there is anything that we can do for you, don't hesitate to give us a call. Thank you!

Property Manager

MOVE-IN PAYMENT SCHEDULE

Date:

The following payments are due from Tenant to cover initial move-in charges at the following address:

1st Month's Rent:

Security Deposit:

Application Fee:

Key Deposit:

Other Deposits:

Tenant agrees to pay the total amount due in the following manner:

$
Date:

$
Date:

$
Date:

Tenant understands that if payment is not made as agreed, the rental/lease agreement becomes void and any money given becomes nonrefundable and is applied to rent for the number of days the premises is held or occupied, as well as to rerenting expenses. Tenant further agrees to immediately turn over rental unit to owner if he or she has already taken possession.

Tenant(s):

Permission Granted: Yes _____   No _____

Owner:

By:

MOVE-IN INSPECTION REPORT

TENANT'S NAME: _____

PROPERTY ADDRESS: _____

KITCHEN
____ Oven
____ Refrigerator
____ Cabinets
____ Countertops
____ Kitchen floor
PLEASE INITIAL _____

BATHROOM
____ Tub and/or shower and sink
____ Medicine chest
____ Vanity
____ Bathroom floor
____ Mirrors
PLEASE INITIAL _____

GENERAL (all rooms)
____ Closets and cabinets are clean
____ Carpet/floor
____ Walls
____ Windows
PLEASE INITIAL_____

Tenant: _____ Date: _____

Landlord: _____ Date: _____

Monthly Inspection Report for Month of _____

Date	Location	Comments

HAPPY HOLIDAYS!

I hope that you and your family had a very happy holiday and have a happy and healthy new year!

Thank you to everyone who has paid their rent on time and to those who have kept their homes nice. I know that your children appreciate it.

There are a few changes for the new year. We are trying to improve our maintenance and response to your service calls. Remember to call us at _____ should you need something. If no one is in, then please leave your name, phone number, address, and what you need. Please be specific.

The owners have instructed me to remind you that all the rent is due on the 1st. You will be charged a late fee after the 5th, and eviction papers must be filed if all the rent is not in by the 11th. All property expenses (including mortgages, taxes, etc.) are due on the 1st and we are not allowed any excuses for late payments. PLEASE SEND ALL YOUR RENT IN BY THE 1ST OF EACH MONTH. This new eviction policy will be effective February 1, 20____.

Do not forget that if you want to plant flowers or bushes around your home, we will reimburse you half the price, once you have planted them and provided us with a receipt.

We hope that you stay with us for a long time. Thank you for all of your help in keeping your home nice.

BEST WISHES for the NEW YEAR!

Your Name

COMPANY ADDRESS

MAINTENANCE GUARANTEE

ATTENTION ALL NEW AND CURRENT RESIDENTS:

We now offer a maintenance guarantee to all residents. To ensure your satisfaction with our rental and the service we provide, we guarantee that all repairs that we are responsible for, as outlined in your lease, will be fixed within 72 hours so that the problem does not continue to create a hardship for you or your family.

If the problem or hardship is not corrected within the 72-hour period, you will have FREE RENT UNTIL THE PROBLEM IS CORRECTED on a per-day basis following the third day, or 72-hour period. Your FREE RENT will be awarded in the form of a rent rebate following the next rental payment received.

NEW RESIDENT: APPROVED BY:

ADDRESS: MOVE-IN DATE:

PREPARATION CHECKLIST FOR COLDER WEATHER

Dear Residents:

Cold weather will soon be upon us, so we'd like to share a checklist that will help keep your heat bills down this winter and make your home warmer and safer for you and your family. Planning ahead can save you money and frustration. Keep in mind that according to the lease agreement, any preventable damage (such as freezing pipes) is your responsibility. So we want you to take all necessary precautions to avoid any unnecessary costs.

Outside Preparation

- Check and close all the vents/windows to the basement/crawl space.
- Unhook your garden hoses.
- Prevent water lines from freezing by wrapping exterior pipes. Even newspapers covered with a waterproof material work.

When the temperature forecast is for extreme cold weather, leave outside faucets running slightly (a small, steady stream of water) but don't allow outside faucets to flow in the street onto sidewalks and other areas where people may walk.

- Check to ensure that the caulking around the outside windows and any weather-stripping around frames are still in place to stop cold air.
- Don't forget to close storm windows. Make sure storm chains, if present, are attached on any storm doors. This prevents strong winds from blowing the door off or damaging the door. Keep the gutters cleaned out. If they are clogged with leaves, the water will overflow and cause the house to rot, or will back up under the roof and into the house.

Reprinted with permission from <www.mrlandlord.com> (Web site for landlords).

Inside Preparation

- Make sure the heat never goes below 50 degrees, even when you are not at home. If the temperature is forecast to drop below freezing, leave at least one inside faucet dripping lukewarm water so that both hot and cold pipes are involved.
- During periods of cold weather, leave cupboard doors open in the kitchen and bathrooms so that pipes inside will be exposed to heat.

If you will be away for more than two consecutive days this winter, please let us know at least one week in advance, so we can check on your property if a sudden freeze occurs. We also want to be able to reach you in case of an emergency.

If you have central heat/air, changing or cleaning the filters monthly can make a big difference in your energy bills. Make sure the attic access door is in place. If you have a fireplace, please clean it. Chimneys need to be cleaned yearly or a chimney fire may occur. Call a professional to do a complete job and check the safety of the chimney.

Test your smoke alarm(s). There are more fires in the winter, and the smoke alarm is one of your best safety features. If you don't have one, or it doesn't work, let us know. Make sure your smoke alarms have a battery and are working. You might also want to consider buying a small fire extinguisher for your kitchen and garage.

Again, this is important for your safety and your family's. Should pipes freeze, don't use open flames to thaw out lines. This may catch the house on fire, or worse, create an explosion caused by expanding steam between two plugs of ice. Pipes don't always burst the first time they freeze. However, should a pipe burst, locate your water shutoff valve, quickly turn it off. If you don't know where the shutoff valve is, let us know now, before any problems occur. If the pipe break is a hot water line, close valve on the top of the water heater. If you think a plumber needs to be called, please use the plumber approved by us.

We greatly appreciate your efforts in helping to make sure your residence is kept warm and as safe as possible during the upcoming winter months. Thank you.

RENTAL UPKEEP VIOLATION NOTICE

DATE:

FROM:

Dear _____,

As you know, we do regular inspections of the rental properties that we manage. Your rental/lease agreement clearly states that you are responsible for the general upkeep of your residence, both in the interior and on the exterior of the property. On our last inspection of your rental property, it was noticed that you have broken your lease by not keeping up with the upkeep of your property. Specifically,

In order to meet the standards necessary to avoid eviction, you must:

Please correct this problem immediately or, if you prefer or if you do not correct the problem quickly, we will hire someone to correct the problem and we will bill you for their services. Remember that this is your obligation.

Thank you for you prompt cooperation. If you have any questions or problems, please do not hesitate to call

Sincerely,

Management

LETTER SENT TO TENANTS WHEN TRASH IS A PROBLEM

What you want to do in this letter is subtly get your point across, like a sledgehammer. The objective is to kind of shame people into being responsible. This letter does just that. See if you agree. Example:

Dear _____,

I have to get this off my chest before I explode! I discovered something very disturbing the other day. So disturbing that it virtually stunned me into silence. "This can't be true," I thought. But, "ugh," it was. I'm talking about TRASH! Trash that brings with it mice, bugs, and other animals. What's more, it looks just awful and makes our place look like a pigsty.

These days, no one should have to live surrounded by trash, bugs, and mice. Besides, trash also brings in dogs that could do harm to our children. It's a real problem. And it's everyone's responsibility to help solve the problem. And I need your help. I really do. Unfortunately, the few offenders who cause this problem have to learn the hard way. So we've decided to charge any tenant $20 (our cost) to clean up a mess that they cause. I can't be any fairer than that.

So please, please, don't make it tough on everyone else and force us to hire an outside party to clean up your trash. My mother used to say, "Cleanliness is next to godliness." She was right, you know. Thanks again for your cooperation. I do appreciate it.

Sincerely,

Property Manager

GARBAGE VIOLATION NOTICE

DATE:

TO:

RE: WE NEED YOUR HELP

As you know, we make periodic inspections of your home and neighborhood. In our last inspection, we noticed that your garbage has been messy. This is in violation of your lease agreement. We realize that it is often difficult to keep garbage in a manner that is not disturbing to neighbors. But keep in mind that messy garbage can attract mice and other animals, such as cats, dogs, and raccoons. It is important to make sure that you keep a tight lid on your garbage or tie it in large plastic bags.

Remember that you are responsible for your own garbage. Because of health risks, it is necessary to keep your garbage in a clean and sanitary manner. Your garbage gets picked up on _____.
Please bring your garbage to the curb the night before.

We also need your assistance in picking up loose papers around and on your property. Unfortunately, papers from adjoining residences are blown on to your property. Even though it may not be your garbage, it is important that you pick it up to keep your property clean. We want you to enjoy your property in a manner that is not offensive to your neighbors. We expect that we will not have to contact you about this problem another time. If Management is forced to contact you again because of more garbage violations, you will place yourself in further default of your lease agreement. Of course, default is a serious matter, which could result in legal action being taken against you and could result in eviction.

In the event you miss the weekly garbage pickup, we urge you to take your own garbage to the town dump immediately, rather than wait until the following week. Garbage that lies around begins to take on an offensive odor and will attract animals. Don't forget . . . Management has the right to terminate your lease if you do not comply with this notice. Also, don't forget to retrieve your garbage cans soon after the garbage is picked up. If you have any questions, or we can be of assistance to you, please call us.

THANKS FOR YOUR HELP!

Management

PERSONAL LETTER TO A PROBLEM TENANT

Dear _____,

I'm worried, Mrs. Smith. I really am. You're a tenant that I really value and enjoy talking to from time to time. I said to my wife the other day that I haven't seen you around for some time, and I can't understand why. I wish I knew the reason. It must be the incident that took place the other evening. Of course, I heard the other side and have yet to hear your side, which is only fair.

Anyway, I do hope that we can get together and discuss the situation, if only because I greatly value you as a tenant and want you to be happy. And, I'm willing to do whatever it takes to get back in your good graces because I do care about you and value our relationship. Please call me to set up a meeting.

Sincerely,

Your Name

RETURNED CHECK NOTICE

A returned check should set off an immediate response. This is a time when you're looking for a tangible result to your letter. A returned check should give you a clue as to what to do next.

Dear (Personalize),

I was contacted by your bank today, and they informed me that your check in the amount of $ _____, which was paid to our company for _____, is now being returned to us. Hopefully, this matter was a simple mistake that can be quickly corrected. Unfortunately, however, because of the returned check, your account balance is past due and delinquent.

I am sorry, but I must notify you that it is critical that you immediately and without delay of any kind make the necessary arrangements to deliver us a money order or a certified check to bring your account up to date.

Here is the way your account currently stands on our books. The total amount that is now due is:

Rent due _____
Loss of discount (if any) _____
Total amount now due _____

Again, I must warn you that the above amount must be paid within _____ days. I do thank you for your cooperation in the matter.

Sincerely,

Your Name

P.S. Please do not delay or ignore this notice. The negative effect that this matter can have on your overall credit rating can be devastating. Bring your money order or certified check in before _____ for your own protection if you want to avoid any added cost of a lawsuit.

PARTIAL PAYMENT ACCEPTANCE NOTICE

DATE:

Dear _____,

We can only accept partial payment if you understand and acknowledge that your rent was due on _____ and that making partial payment does not waive our right, according to the lease agreement, to continue with legal proceedings without further notice. We do appreciate your efforts in fulfilling your obligation and it will help with your credit standing with our company. If your partial payment proposal is satisfactory, we will work with you. However, if this occurs more often or if you fail to do as you promise, we will immediately begin legal proceedings without further notice, leading to your eviction.

As you know, your total rent now past due is $_____, which includes _____.

How do you propose to pay this complete amount?

Date: $

Date: $

Please sign below, giving your agreement to the above terms and acknowledging that you understand that you have violated the lease agreement and partial payment does not stop us from continuing legal proceedings. Should you choose to ignore this notice to you, we will begin legal proceedings immediately. Please call us if you have any questions.

Sincerely,

Management

Tenant Signature:

Date:

Reprinted with permission from <www.mrlandlord.com> (Web site for landlords).

PAY RENT OR QUIT LETTER

This is a get-tough letter. It's the time to be serious and forceful. It's the time to enforce your rental agreement. It is not a time to back down. I repeat: It is not a time to fall for a sob story. It is a time to see that you're paid for services the tenant has received and rent that you are legitimately owed.

Conventional thinking advises an alternative arrangement whereby you continue to allow the delinquent tenant to remain—assuming he or she will pay you cash every month, plus additional cash for a portion (e.g., 25%) of the outstanding balance. This system, proponents claim, clears up an otherwise endangered balance and the tenant arranges for an uninterrupted flow of cash until the account is cleared. The drawback: It's too easy to fall into the sob story trap with more than one. And then your entire cash-flow situation can begin to start hemorrhaging.

A newspaper article in the Minneapolis Star Tribune *(4/18/94) ended a column on the past-due subject with this question: "Would you lend a friend money if he hadn't paid off what he'd borrowed before? Of course, you wouldn't. The same rule applies to business." That pretty much says it all.*

Another suggestion: Send the letter below by registered mail. Incidentally, including the date, day, and time at the heading makes your letter appear even more imposing.

Date:

Dear _____,

I have registered this letter to make sure that it is delivered to you personally. The reason: In the event of a lawsuit being filed against you, your attorney cannot say that you have not had sufficient notice. Fact is, I was down at the courthouse the other day and noticed how unhappy a tenant was when settlement of his case ended. This man owed his landlord $530 in back rent. By the time the judgments and lawyers' fees had been issued, it cost him $1,139.90. So, if you are not willing to take the necessary steps to pay the rent that you owe of $ _____ from the period of _____ to _____, plus a late fee of $ _____ for a total amount of $ _____, we will have to start legal proceedings.

We are not unreasonable people, but we do insist that you live by the rental agreement that you signed. Our other tenants do, and we make no exceptions regardless of your circumstances. In order to prevent legal proceedings beginning by _____, you will have to act quickly, though, and we will require some evidence that you are going to pay the amount due. Otherwise, my attorney will cancel your rental agreement (as it states) and you will be required to leave the premises immediately. That alone could cost you a great deal of your hard-earned money, as well. We expect to hear from you by _____. The rest is up to you. After that, the legal action and its expense go into effect. Why not act right now?

Insistently,

Your Name

PAY RENT OR QUIT (Option 2)

Dear _____,

You are hereby notified that the rent for the premises now occupied by you, located at _____, is now PAST DUE! Your last payment was due on _____. Your account is now delinquent in the amount of $ _____. This is rent for the period from _____ to _____.

Please send payment immediately. You are required by law to pay the past-due amount in full within _____ days. If we have not received it within _____ days, the lease agreement (as it so states) will be terminated. You will be required to vacate immediately and deliver up possession of said premises. If you fail to pay or vacate, legal proceedings will be instituted against you to recover possession of said premises, unpaid rent, plus damages, court costs, and attorney fees.

DATED THIS _____ DAY OF: _____, 20____

OWNER/MANAGER

PAY RENT OR QUIT (Option 3)

DATE:

TO: _____
       Tenant

       _____
       Address

Notice to you and all others in possession of the below premises, that you are hereby notified to vacate, quit, and deliver up the premises you hold as our tenant, namely: (Describe premises) _____

_____

You are to deliver up said premises on or within _____ days of receipt of this notice, pursuant to applicable state law.

This notice is provided due to nonpayment of rent. The present rent arrearage is in the amount of $ _____, according to the below account.

You may reinstate your account by full payment within _____ days as provided under the terms of your tenancy or by applicable state law. In the event you fail to bring your rent payments current or to vacate the premises, we shall immediately take legal action to evict you and to recover rents and damages for the unlawful retention of said premises together with such future rents as may be due us for breach of your tenancy agreements.

Owner   _____   By   _____
        Agent

Address _____

PROOF OF SERVICE

I, the undersigned, being at least eighteen years of age, declare under penalty of perjury that I served within notice to pay rent or quit tenancy, of which this is a true copy, on the above named tenant in the manner indicated below on _____, 20____.

_____ I personally delivered a copy of the notice to tenant.

_____ I mailed a true copy of the notice to tenant by certified mail.

_____ I mailed a true copy of this notice to tenant by first-class mail.

Executed on _____, 20____, at   By _____

30 DAYS' NOTICE TO TERMINATE TENANCY

TO:

You are hereby notified that your tenancy at the dwelling now occupied by you, located at: _____ will end as of _____.

This is to give you a minimum of 30 days' advance notice requiring you to deliver up possession, vacate, and remove your belongings on or before stated date. Failure to vacate will result in legal proceedings against you to recover possession as well as additional rent and damages and court costs for remaining unlawfully within the dwelling. Please contact our office if you have any questions regarding this notice and to receive information on the procedure for getting your security deposit back. Thank you for your cooperation.

Sincerely,

Rental Manager   Dated:

FORM INDICATING GROUNDS FOR EVICTION

For Nonpayment _____
Suit on a lease for accrued rent, late charges, damages, and a reasonable attorney's fee.

For Other Breach of Lease _____
Suit on lease for accrued rent, late charges, damages, and a reasonable attorney's fee or the alternative on a three/fourteen-day notice of termination of tenancy.

(Circle three or fourteen, if we are evicting on a three-day notice or a fourteen-day notice.)

THE FOLLOWING INFORMATION IS VITAL TO
<u>RECOVER ALL MONIES DUE THE COMPLEX</u>

Did Lessee give 30 days' notice? _____

Did Lessee return keys? _____ Date returned _____

Date vacated _____

Rent paid thru _____

Date unit rerented _____

Security deposit _____ Amount _____

Cleaning fee _____ Amount _____

Pet fee _____ Amount _____

RENT OWED   (MONTH)   Amount

_____   _____

_____   _____

_____   _____

LATE CHARGES   (MONTH)   Amount

_____   _____

_____   _____

_____   _____

OTHER CHARGES   (MONTH)   Amount

_____   _____

_____   _____

_____   _____

TENANT PLANNING TO MOVE LETTER

Every so often, a tenant will threaten to move over some trivial mis-understanding, or whatever. They don't realize the expense of such a move. This letter gives them a touch of reality as to what a move involves, expensewise.

Dear _____,

I understand that you're thinking seriously of moving. So I took the liberty of putting together a checklist of the costs you'll have to pay, if you are indeed prepared to move out. I've always felt that I would like to know up front what my entire expenses are going to be before I make a move. So I thought it would be helpful if I included the following checklist I've used in the past so that you don't underestimate the expense of moving. Quite frankly, it can be pretty costly. I've found that out myself the hard way.

Something else: If you do decide to stay, I would certainly appreciate it if you would let us know before I rent the space to someone else. I really would feel terrible if that happened because I've always valued you as a tenant. Anyway, here is the moving checklist that I use—I hope it helps you know in advance the money you will have to come up with:

1. A security deposit
2. Income lost (time off of work)
3. First (and possibly the second) month's rent in advance
4. The actual moving cost and packing and unpacking cost
5. Deposit on utilities
6. New telephone installation
7. Any items broken and replaced during the move
8. Any other items you may need in the new location

I suggest that you take the same precautions that I do when I move. So my advice is to add up items 1 through 8 to get an idea of the total dollar amount that you'll have to come up with immediately. In any event, I hope this checklist has been helpful. If I can help out in any other way, please let me know.

Sincerely,

Your Name

P.S. Again, please let me know in the next ten days what you decide, so that I don't lease your unit to someone else without your knowing about it in advance. But you really ought to stay, because otherwise somebody else is going to take it, and we don't want to lose you. It will cost you $1,500 to $2,000 to move; we hope you decide not to.

VACANCY MAKEOVER CHECKLIST

❑ Check and test all wall receptacles and switches. One faulty switch will affect the overall safety of the electrical system.

❑ Turn on/off all faucets. Check for leaks, also around the tub, showerheads, and under sinks.

❑ Flush toilets. Make sure they are functioning properly—no leaks around bottom—they maintain water, and shut off properly.

❑ Close and open all doors, exterior, interior, sliding, and closets. Check doorstops.

❑ If drapes are provided, clean or order replacements.

❑ Clean and vacuum all carpets.

❑ Exterminate all pests.

❑ Replace lightbulbs if out. Good lighting helps show vacant units.

❑ Clean (in, behind, and under) and check all appliances. Make sure all appliances are running effectively.

❑ Make sure all countertops, drawers, and cabinets are clean. Remove old shelf paper.

❑ Check to see that all hardware is in place.

❑ Make bathrooms shine (tubs, sink, mirrors, all tile, medicine cabinets, and vanities). Remove any decals. Paint if necessary.

Reprinted with permission from <www.mrlandlord.com> (Web site for landlords).

❑ Make sure all bathroom details are in place (towel bars, toilet paper holders, soap dishes).

❑ Check condition of paint on all interior walls/ceilings. Paint if necessary. Fill in any holes.

❑ Clean and shine all vinyl flooring.

❑ Clean all windows and mirrors. Replace any broken or scratched windows. Check to see if all screens are in place and whether they are torn.

❑ Check heating units and air conditioners, including replacing filters.

❑ Remove all debris or personal items left.

❑ Put air freshener in place.

❑ Sweep entryways and wash off front of building/house. Does front porch need painting?

❑ Rekey all locks and ensure all are working properly. See if any window locks are needed.

❑ Is exterior of premises clean and neat? Does grass need cutting, or other landscaping needs?

Checklist Completed:

Date:

RETURN OF SECURITY DEPOSIT UPON MOVE-OUT

Moving out will be a hectic time for you. We want it to go smoothly and we want to return your security deposit as soon as possible. Some people prefer to do some or all of their own move-out cleaning, maintenance, and repair. However, in the event you simply don't have the time or energy to make all of the necessary repairs or clean up the residence, we can do it for you for a fee.

Why not let us concentrate on moving you out, so you can concentrate on moving into your new home. We can ensure that the home meets with the owner's high standards. The best part is that our services can be paid for from your security deposit, so you won't have any more out-of-pocket expenses. In the unlikely event our fee exceeds the amount of your security deposit, you would of course be charged the difference.

For your planning purposes, here are minimum-charge rates on some of the most common items:

CLEANING:

Stove or Oven
Cabinets
Toilets
Vanity
Windows
Carpets
Refrigerator
Countertops
Shower/Tub
Floor (bathrooms)

Bedroom Floors
Closets
Kitchen Sink
Floor (kitchen)
Medicine Cabinet
Trash Removal (per room)
Tile Cleaning
Extensive Cleaning
    (any room per hour)

DAMAGE:

Negligent Soiling or Damage to Walls	per room
Removal of Wall Covering	per hour
Nail Holes or Other Small Holes	each
Larger Holes (½″ or larger)	each
Cigarette Burns in Carpeting	each
Rugs/Pads Requiring Replacement	per sq. yd.
Lightbulb Replacement	each
Missing Keys	each
Lock Replacement	each
Lawn Maintenance	minimum
Missing Screens	each
Broken Windows	each
Door Damage/Replacement	each

Sample Lease and Addenda

Lease Agreement
Security Deposit Policy
Pet Agreement
Discount Policy for Prepayment of Rent
Transfer Cancellation Privilege
No-Fault Maintenance Plan
Sample Disclosure Format for Superior Properties Corp.
  Disclosure of Information on Lead-Based Paint and
  Lead-Based-Paint Hazards
Payment Policy
Option to Purchase Real Estate

LEASE AGREEMENT

1. **PARTIES:** The parties to this agreement are **Superior Proper-ties Corporation,** hereinafter referred to as "Landlord," and _____, and _____, here-inafter referred to as "Tenant(s)." All adult occupants of the sub-ject premises must sign this Lease Agreement and each will be jointly and severally liable under the terms and conditions of said Agreement. Additional occupants of the premises will be _____ _____ (Age_____); _____ (Age____); and _____ (Age_____) only.

2. **PROPERTY:** Landlord hereby lets the following property to Ten-ant for the term of this agreement; the property located at and known as: _____, in _____, _____, Tennessee.
        (City)   (County)

3. **TERM:** The term of the Agreement shall be for _____ _____, beginning on _____ and ending on _____.

4. **RENT:** The monthly/weekly rental for said property shall be $ _____ per month/week. One full month's/week's rent shall be paid upon execution of this Agreement. Rent for the second month/week is the prorated amount of $ _____, and is due and payable on the _____ day of _____, 200_____. The remaining payments are to be paid consecutively on the first day of each month/week (Saturday) at such place as the Landlord shall direct. NOTICE OF TERMINATION OF TENANCY UNDER LEASE AGREEMENT FOR NONPAYMENT OF RENT IS HEREBY SPECIFICALLY WAIVED.

5. **LATE CHARGES:** Any rent installment that is paid more than five (5) days after its due date shall include a late charge of 10% (ten percent) of the rent installment. Said late charges shall become a separate portion of rent due under the Terms and Con-ditions of this Lease.

6. **RETURNED CHECK CHARGES:** A charge of $25.00 shall be paid by Tenant for any check that is returned unpaid. Upon return or dishonor of any check tendered as payment of rent, late charges will be assessed as if no rental payment was attempted.

7. **UTILITIES, APPLIANCES, AND OTHER ITEMS FURNISHED BY LANDLORD:**

Utilities shall be paid by the party indicated on the following chart:

	LANDLORD	TENANT
Electricity	_____	_____
Gas	_____	_____
Water	_____	_____
Garbage	_____	_____
Other	_____	_____

Appliances furnished to Tenant by Landlord:

	YES	NO
Refrigerator	_____	_____
Stove	_____	_____
Air conditioner	_____	_____
Dishwasher	_____	_____

Yard care shall be the responsibility of the Landlord/Tenant.

When electricity, gas, or water is to be furnished by Landlord, Tenant agrees not to use any supplemental heating or air-conditioning units, clothes or dishwashing machines, or clothes dryers, other than those furnished by Landlord and above listed. Due to the high utility costs involving use of such units or appliances, tenant agrees to obtain prior written approval before using or connecting such supplemental units or appliances.

Tenant agrees that any unauthorized use of supplemental heating or air-conditioning units, clothes or dishwashing machines, or clothes dryers, other than those furnished by Landlord and above listed, shall increase the monthly/weekly rental for the subject property at the rate of $ _____ per month or per week. Said increase shall be automatic upon discovery of any of the above mentioned units or appliances, without any notice required, and shall continue for the full term of this Lease. Said increase shall become a portion of rent due under the Terms and Conditions of this Agreement.

8. **USE OF PROPERTY, OCCUPANTS, AND GUESTS:** Tenant shall use the subject property for residential purposes only. The property shall be occupied only by those Tenants listed in item one (1): PARTIES, of this Lease.

9. **TENANT'S DUTY TO MAINTAIN PREMISES:** Tenant shall keep the dwelling unit in a clean and sanitary condition and shall otherwise comply with all state and local laws requiring tenants to maintain rented premises. If damage to the dwelling unit other than normal wear and tear is caused by acts of negligence of Tenant or others occupying the premises under his/her control, Landlord may cause such repairs to be made, and Tenant shall be liable to Landlord for any reasonable expense thereby incurred by Landlord.

10. **ALTERATIONS:** No alteration, addition, or improvements shall be made by Tenant in or to the dwelling unit without the prior written consent of Landlord. Such consent shall be totally at Landlord's option.

11. **NOISE:** Tenant agrees not to allow on the premises any excessive noise, or other activity, which disturbs the peace and quiet of others.

12. **INSPECTION BY LANDLORD:** The Tenant agrees to allow Landlord to enter the subject premises in order to inspect the premises, make necessary or agreed-upon repairs, decorations, alterations, or improvements, supply necessary or agreed-upon services, or exhibit the dwelling unit to prospective or actual purchasers, mortgagees, tenants, workmen, or contractors. The

Landlord may enter the dwelling unit without consent of Tenant in case of emergency.

13. **SECURITY DEPOSIT:** Tenant agrees to deposit with Landlord, upon execution of the Lease contract, receipt of which is hereby acknowledged, the sum of _____. This deposit is held as security against any damage to the entire property, including but not limited to furniture, appliances, fixtures, and carpet; and against Tenant vacating the entire premises prior to the termination date of this Lease, or failing to perform any and all the covenants herein. Said deposit is neither an advance rental payment nor a bonus to the Landlord, and Landlord agrees that if all the covenants imposed upon Tenant have been fulfilled, Landlord shall refund said deposit by mail to the address furnished by the Tenant, after the premises have been vacated by Tenant and inspected by Landlord as provided by statute. Said deposit shall be deposited in _____ Bank.

14. **LIEN:** The Tenant hereby gives Landlord a lien upon all his personal property situated upon said premises, including all furniture and household furnishings. This lien is for the rent agreed to be paid hereunder, for any damage caused by Tenant beyond normal wear and tear, and for court costs and attorneys' fees incurred under the Terms and Conditions of this Agreement.

15. **SUBLEASING:** Tenant shall not assign this Agreement or sublet the dwelling unit without prior written consent of Landlord. Such consent shall be totally at Landlord's option.

16. **PERSONAL INJURY AND PROPERTY DAMAGE:** Subject to standards required by law, neither Landlord nor its principal shall be liable to Tenant, his family, employees, or guests, for any damage to person or property caused by the acts or omissions of other Tenants or other persons, whether such persons be off the property of Landlord or on the property with or without permission of Landlord; nor shall Landlord be liable for losses or damages from theft, fire, water, rain, storm, explosion, sonic boom, or other

causes whatsoever, nor shall Landlord be liable for loss or damages resulting from failure, interruption, or malfunctions in the utilities provided to Tenant under this Lease Agreement; nor shall Landlord be liable for injuries elsewhere on the premises.

LANDLORD IS NOT RESPONSIBLE FOR, AND WILL NOT PROVIDE, FIRE OR CASUALTY INSURANCE FOR THE TENANT'S PERSONAL PROPERTY.

In further consideration of this Agreement, Tenant agrees that, subject to standards required by law, Landlord does not warrant the condition of the premises in any respect, and his liability for any injury to the Tenant, his family, agent, or those claiming under him, or those on the premises by his or their invitation, shall be limited to injuries arising from such defects that are unknown by claimant and are known to Landlord or are willfully concealed by him. Additionally, Tenant has inspected the premises and binds himself to hold Landlord harmless against any and all claims for damages arising from those who sustain injuries upon the above-leased premises, during the term of this Lease, or any extension thereof.

17. **IN CASE OF MALFUNCTION OF EQUIPMENT, DAMAGE BY FIRE, WATER, OR ACT OF GOD:** Tenant shall notify Landlord immediately of malfunction of equipment, damage by fire, water, or act of God and Landlord shall repair the damage with reasonable promptness, or if the premises are deemed by the Landlord to be damaged so much as to be unfit for occupancy, or if the Landlord decides not to repair or restore the building, this Lease shall terminate. If the Lease is so terminated, rent will be prorated on a daily basis so that Tenant will pay only to the date of the damage, and the remainder of the month will be refunded.

18. **PETS:** Tenant shall not permit a pet to live on the premises without signing and complying with the provisions of a separately negotiated Pet Agreement. All pets are subject to visual inspec-

tion and approval of Landlord at such times as Landlord may direct during normal working hours.

19. **TERMINATION—ALL TENANTS PLEASE TAKE NOTICE!** At least thirty (30) days prior to the termination date of this Lease Agreement, Tenant must give Landlord written notice of his intent to vacate the subject premises. Failure of Tenant to give Landlord said notice of intent to vacate the subject premises will cause Landlord to treat tenant as a holdover in accordance with item twenty (20.), **HOLDOVER,** of this Lease Agreement, no matter if Tenant continues to occupy the premises or not.

Upon proper termination or expiration of this Agreement, Tenant shall vacate the premises, remove all personal property belonging to him, and leave the premises as clean as he found them.

20. **HOLDOVER:** If Tenant holds over upon termination or expiration of this Agreement and/or Landlord accepts Tenant's tender of the monthly rent provided by this Agreement, this Agreement shall continue to be binding on the parties as a month-to-month agreement under the same Terms and Conditions as herein contained.

21. **ATTORNEYS' FEES:** Violation of any of the conditions of this Agreement shall be sufficient cause for eviction from said premises. Tenants agree to pay all costs of such action or cost of collection of damages as a result of Tenant's breach of this Agreement, including reasonable attorneys' fees.

22. **NOTICES:** All notices provided for by this Agreement shall be in writing and shall be given to the other party as follows: to Tenant, at the premises; to Landlord, at P.O. BOX 128186, Nashville, TN 37212-8186.

23. **MAINTENANCE REQUESTS:** Except in emergencies, all requests for maintenance must be made in writing to Landlord, at

the following address: P.O. BOX 128186, Nashville, TN 37212-8186.

24. **ABSENCE OR ABANDONMENT:** The Tenant must notify the Landlord of any extended absence from the premises in excess of seven (7) days. Notice shall be given on or before the first day of any extended absence. The Tenant's unexplained and/or extended absence from the premises for (30) days or more without payment of rent as due shall be prima facie evidence of abandonment. The Landlord is then expressly authorized to enter, remove, and store all personal items belonging to Tenant. If Tenant does not claim said personal property within an additional thirty (30) days, Landlord may sell or dispose of said personal property and apply the proceeds of said sale to the unpaid rents, damages, storage fees, sale costs, and attorneys' fees. Any unclaimed balance held by the Landlord for a period of six (6) months shall be forfeited to the Landlord.

25. **TERMINATION FOR VIOLENT OR DANGEROUS BEHAVIOR:** Landlord shall terminate this Lease Agreement within three (3) days from the date written notice is delivered to the Tenant if the Tenant or any other persons on the premises with the Tenant's consent willfully or intentionally commit a violent act or behave in a manner that constitutes or threatens to be a real and present danger to the health, safety, or welfare of the life or property of others.

26. **BREACH OF LEASE:** If there is any other material noncompliance of the Lease Agreement by the Tenant, not previously specifically mentioned, or a noncompliance materially affecting health and safety, the Landlord may deliver a written notice to the Tenant specifying the acts and omissions constituting the breach, and that the Lease Agreement will terminate upon a date not less than thirty (30) days after receipt of the notice. If the breach is not remedied in fourteen (14) days, the Lease Agreement shall terminate as provided in the notice subject to the following: If the breach is remediable by repairs or the payment of damages or otherwise

and the Tenant adequately remedies the breach prior to the date specified in the notice, the rental agreement will not terminate.

If the same act or omission that constituted a prior noncompliance, of which notice was given, recurs within six (6) months, the Landlord may terminate the Lease Agreement upon at least (14) days' written notice specifying the breach and the date of termination of the Lease Agreement.

27. **RULES AND REGULATIONS:** Tenant has read and agrees to abide by all Rules and Regulations of the Landlord as they presently exist or as they may be amended at Landlord's sole discretion. Said Rules and Regulations are attached hereto and are herein incorporated by reference.

28. **ALTERATIONS OR CHANGE IN THIS AGREEMENT:** It is expressly understood by Landlord and Tenant that the Terms and Conditions herein set out cannot be changed or modified, except in writing. Tenant understands that neither Tenant nor Landlord or any of Landlord's agents have the authority to modify this Lease Agreement except with a written instrument signed by all parties.

29. **APPLICATION:** Tenant's Application is an important part of this Lease, incorporated by reference and made a part hereof. Any misrepresentations, misleading or false statements made by Tenant and later discovered by the Landlord shall, at the option of the Landlord, void this Lease Agreement.

30. **SAVINGS CLAUSE:** If any provision of this Lease is determined to be in conflict with the law, thereby making said provision null and void, the nullity shall not affect the other provisions of this Lease, which can be given effect without the void provision, and to this end the provisions of the Lease are severable.

31. **TENANTS ARE RESPONSIBLE FOR THEIR OWN SECURITY:** Tenant hereby states that he has inspected the subject premises and has determined to his satisfaction that the smoke detectors,

door locks and latches, window locks and latches, and any other security devices within the subject premises are adequate and in proper working order. Tenant acknowledges that Landlord is under no obligation or duty to inspect, test, or repair smoke detectors during Tenant's occupancy. Further, Tenant acknowledges that Landlord is under no obligation or duty to inspect, test, or repair any other security device unless and until Landlord has received written notice of disrepair of the device.

Tenant further acknowledges that neither Landlord nor his agents or representatives guarantee, warrant, or assume the personal security of Tenant. Tenant further acknowledges and understands that Tenant's personal safety and security is primarily Tenant's responsibility. In particular, Tenant recognizes that Tenant is in the best position to determine and foresee risks of loss and to protect himself and his property against such losses. In this regard, Tenant recognizes that any of Landlord's efforts are voluntary and not obligatory.

32. **ADDITIONAL TERMS AND CONDITIONS:** Additional paragraphs _____ through _____ are attached hereto and are part of this Lease Agreement.

Wherefore, we the undersigned do hereby execute and agree to this Lease Agreement, this _____ day of _____ , 20___.

President, Superior Properties Corp. _____
LANDLORD TENANT SS#_____

_____ _____
LANDLORD/MANAGER TENANT SS#_____

RULES AND REGULATIONS
(Referred to in, and made a part of, the Parties' Lease Agreement)

1. No signs, notices, or advertisements shall be attached to or displayed by Tenant on or about said premises. Additionally, no antenna or satellite dish shall be attached to or displayed on or about the premises.

2. Profane, obscene, loud, or boisterous language, or unseemly behavior and conduct, is absolutely prohibited, and Tenant obligates himself, and those under him, not to do or permit to be done anything that will annoy, harass, embarrass, or inconvenience any of the other tenants or occupants in the subject or adjoining premises.

3. No motor vehicle shall be kept upon the property that is unlicensed, inoperable, or in damaged condition. Damaged condition includes, but is not limited to, flat tires. Any such vehicle that remains on the property for more than ten (10) days after notice to remove same has been placed on subject vehicle shall be towed by a wrecker and stored with a wrecker service at the tenant's and/or the vehicle owner's expense.

4. In keeping with Fire Safety Standards, all motorized vehicles including motorcycles must be parked outside. No motorized vehicles shall be parked in any building structure on the property except authorized garage spaces.

5. In accordance with Fire Safety Standards and other safety regulations, no Tenant shall maintain, or allow to be maintained, any auxiliary heating unit, air-conditioning units, or air filtering units without prior inspection and written approval of Landlord.

6. The sound of musical instruments, radios, televisions, phonographs, and singing shall at all times be limited in volume to a point that is not objectionable to other tenants or occupants in the subject or adjoining premises.

7. Only persons employed by Landlord or his agent shall adjust or have anything to do with the heating or air-conditioning plants or with the repair or adjustment of any plumbing, stove, refrigerator, dishwasher, or any other equipment that is furnished by Landlord or is part of the subject premises.

8. No awning, venetian blinds, or window guards shall be installed, except where prior approval is given by the Landlord.

9. Tenant shall not alter, replace, or add locks or bolts or install any other attachments, such as door knockers, upon any door, except where prior approval is given by the Landlord.

10. No defacement of the interior or exterior of the buildings or the surrounding grounds will be tolerated.

11. If furnished by Landlord, garbage disposal shall only be used in accordance with the disposal guidelines. All refuse shall be, in a timely manner, removed from the premises and placed outside in receptacles.

12. No spikes, hooks, or nails shall be driven into the walls, ceiling or woodwork of the leased premises without consent of Landlord. No crating of or boxing of furniture or other articles will be allowed within the leased premises.

13. It is specifically understood that Landlord reserves solely to itself the right to alter, amend, modify, and add rules to this Lease.

14. It is understood and agreed that Landlord shall not be responsible for items stored in storage areas.

15. Landlord has the right to immediately remove combustible material from the premises or any storage area.

16. Landlord will furnish one (1) key for each outside door of the premises. All keys must be returned to Landlord upon termination of the occupancy.

17. Lavatories, sinks, toilets, and all water and plumbing apparatuses shall be used only for the purpose for which they were constructed. Sweepings, rubbish, rags, ashes, or other foreign substances shall not be thrown therein. Any damage to such apparatuses, and the cost of clearing plumbing resulting from misuse, shall be the sole responsibility of, and will be borne by, Tenant.

_____

TENANT   TENANT

_____

TENANT   TENANT

SECURITY DEPOSIT POLICY

Refund of the security deposit referred to in the attached Lease Agreement is subject to compliance with all six (6) of the following provisions: That a full term of the lease has expired and

1. That thirty (30) days' written notice is given, prior to vacating the subject premises at the end of said full term and;

2. That there are no damages to Landlord's property, including but not limited to furniture, appliances, carpet, drapes, blinds, and floor coverings, and;

3. That the entire apartment, including range, refrigerator, bathrooms, closets, and cupboards, is clean and;

4. That no late charges, delinquent rents, or fees for the damages remain unpaid and;

5. That all keys, including mailbox keys, are returned to the Landlord.

The following questions and answers are for the purpose of eliminating misunderstandings concerning the security deposit:

1. **Question: What charges will be deducted from the deposit if Tenant has failed to comply with all of the above listed six (6) conditions?**

Answer: The cost of all material and labor for cleaning the apartment and making repairs, all delinquent payments and fees, and all rental income lost as a result of Tenant vacating the premises prior to the termination date of his lease, or during any holdover period.

2. **Question: What should Tenant be careful to avoid?**

Answer:

    (a) Damage to property, furniture, walls and wall coverings, appliances, carpet, drapes/blinds, and floor coverings. Departing Tenant will be held responsible for all damages beyond normal wear and tear.

    (b) Dirty appliances: Be sure to clean range and refrigerator.

3. **Question: How is the Security Deposit returned?**

Answer. If Tenant has complied with all the terms and conditions concerning the Security Deposit, the deposit will be returned by check mailed to a forwarding address furnished to Landlord by Tenant.

NOTE: The Security Deposit may not be applied to the last monthly rental, or to any other rent payment!

---------------------------------   ---------------------------------

TENANT   TENANT

---------------------------------   ---------------------------------

TENANT   TENANT

PET AGREEMENT

Tenant agrees that only the pet described and named below will occupy premises. No additional or different pet is authorized under this Agreement.

Tenant agrees that said pet shall be kept under the direct control of Tenant at all times.

Tenant agrees that if pet becomes annoying, bothersome, or in any way a nuisance to other tenants, or to the community, Tenant shall immediately upon notice from Landlord remove the pet from the premises, or vacate the premises.

Tenant agrees to pay the Landlord, upon execution of this supplementary Pet Agreement, the additional sum of $_____. This amount is NONREFUNDABLE, and does not prohibit Landlord from recovery of any and all damages to the subject premises, caused by said pet.

Landlord sets a limit of _____ lbs. for the subject pet.

Type of Pet: _____Breed: _____
Name of Pet: _____Age: _____ Weight:_____
Color of Pet: _____ License #: _____

All Tenants residing in the unit must sign this Pet Agreement.

DATE: _____

BY: _____
LANDLORD

_____
TENANT

_____
TENANT

_____
TENANT

DISCOUNT POLICY FOR PREPAYMENT OF RENT

For, and in consideration of, Tenant paying rent by the first (1st) day of the month in which said rent is due, Tenant may take a discount of $_____ for that specific month. To receive said discount, rent must be received by Landlord or postmarked no later than the first day of the month in which said rent is due.

EXAMPLE:
     $425.00 (actual rent)
     – 25.00 (discount for prepayment)
     $400.00

_____

LANDLORD

_____

TENANT

_____

TENANT

_____

TENANT

_____

TENANT

TRANSFER CANCELLATION PRIVILEGE

For, and in consideration of, $ _____ cash in hand that is paid, receipt of which is hereby acknowledged, it is agreed that this transfer cancellation privilege shall become a part of Tenant's Lease Agreement. It is understood and agreed that if Tenant is transferred by his employer from this city to another city during the term of this Lease contract, Tenant may secure a release from this Lease contract by giving a thirty (30) days' written notice through presentation of a letter from his employer stating the date and new location of the transfer.

Additional consideration for this right of cancellation is for the forfeiture of all deposits, even if there has been no damage to Landlord's property. It is expressly understood that release may be obtained only after compliance with all other provisions of the Lease Agreement.

_____
LANDLORD/LESSOR

_____
TENANT

_____
TENANT

_____
TENANT

_____
TENANT

NO-FAULT MAINTENANCE PLAN

It is expressly agreed that the rental required in this Lease is a reduced figure, reflecting Tenant's willingness to accept the responsibilities outlined in this additional paragraph. Tenant agrees that he has inspected the subject premises, furnishings, and equipment, and that the same now are in good order and condition, except as herein noted.

Therefore, Tenant agrees to be responsible for all plumbing repairs, including but not limited to leaks, stoppage, frozen pipes and water damage, appliances, furnishings, equipment, and the entire premises, including but not limited to glass, screens, and doors.

Further, Tenant will keep the grounds clean and neat, and free of trash and debris. This includes mowing the lawn and trimming of trees and shrubs.

The parties realize that this additional paragraph amends and modifies other language in the attached Lease Agreement form, the Rules and Regulations that are a part of that, and Landlord's duty to maintain the subject premises.

NOTES: _____

_____

_____

_____
LANDLORD

_____
TENANT

_____
TENANT

_____
TENANT

SAMPLE DISCLOSURE FORMAT FOR SUPERIOR PROPERTIES CORP. DISCLOSURE OF INFORMATION ON LEAD-BASED PAINT AND LEAD-BASED-PAINT HAZARDS

Lead Warning Statement

Housing built before 1978 may contain lead-based paint. Lead from paint, paint chips, and dust can pose health hazards if not taken care of properly. Lead exposure is especially harmful to young children and pregnant women. Before renting pre-1978 housing, landlords must disclose the presence of known lead-based paint and lead-based-paint hazards in the dwelling. Tenants must also receive a federally approved pamphlet on lead poisoning prevention. Lessor's Disclosure (initial)

_____ (a) Presence of lead-based paint or lead-based-paint hazards (check one below):

❏ Known lead-based paint or lead-based-paint hazards are present in the housing (explain).

_____

_____

❏ Lessor has no knowledge of lead-based paint and/or lead-based-paint hazards in the housing.

_____ (b) Records and reports available to the lessor (check one below):

❏ Lessor has provided the lessee with all available records and reports pertaining to lead-based paint and/or lead-based-paint hazards in the housing (list documents below).

_____

_____

❏ Lessor has no reports or records pertaining to lead-based paint and/or lead-based-paint hazards in the housing.

Lessee's Acknowledgment (initial)

_____ (c) Lessee has received copies of all information listed above.

_____ (d) Lessee has received the pamphlet *Protect Your Family from Lead in Your Home.*

Agent's Acknowledgment (initial)

_____ (e) Agent has **informed** the lessor of the lessor's obligations under 42 U.S.C. 4582(d) and is aware of his/her responsibility to ensure compliance.

Certification of Accuracy

The following parties have reviewed the information above and certify, to the best of their knowledge,

that the information provided by the signatory is true and accurate.

Lessor	Date	Lessor	Date
Lessee	Date	Lessee	Date
Agent	Date	Agent	Date

PAYMENT POLICY

I, _____, understand that
all rent is due on the

- 1st of the month.
- Rent is late on the 6th.
- Eviction begins on the 11th of the month. No exceptions.

I understand and agree that my rent will be paid on time.

_____   _____
Tenant's Signature   Date

_____   _____
Tenant's Signature   Date

OPTION TO PURCHASE REAL ESTATE

This agreement, made this _____ day of _____, 20___, by and between _____, hereinafter called Optioner, and _____, hereinafter called Optionee. Witnesseth, that for and in consideration of the sum of _____ dollars ($_____) paid by Optionee to Optioner, the receipt whereof is hereby acknowledged, the Optioner hereby gives and grants unto the Optionee's heirs, personal representatives, and assigns, the right of purchasing, on or before the _____ day of _____, 20___, the following described real estate situated in _____ County, State, to-wit:

_____

for the purchase price of _____ Dollars ($ _____).

Shall be paid as follows _____.

If the Optionee elects to purchase the said real estate pursuant to this Option, Optionee shall give notice to such Optioner, at _____ _____, on or before the _____ day of _____, 20____.

If the Optionee shall so elect to purchase said real estate, and shall give of such election as herein provided within the time required, and shall tender the required amount of cash, and a real estate contract or other security to Optioner, on the real estate hereinabove particularly described, then Optioner agrees to convey the real estate to Optionee heirs, and assigns, by warranty deed, free and clear of all liens, encumbrances, or taxes to the date of closing of the purchase. Optioner further agrees, that upon such election by Optionee, to deliver to Optionee, within 30 days after receipt of such written notice of election to purchase, a policy of title insurance in the full sum of the purchase price showing merchantable title to said real estate.

If the Optionee does not exercise the privilege of purchase given and does not fully perform the conditions herein within the time herein stated, the privilege shall wholly cease and terminate and the sum of

_____ dollars ($_____), herein paid by Optionee, shall be retained by Optioner.

The right by either party to terminate this agreement for failure to perform or observe the obligations, agreements, or covenants of this agreement, the party at fault shall pay all reasonable attorneys' fees and expenses of the other party.

This agreement constitutes the entire agreement of the parties hereto and may not be modified except by a written document signed by all parties.

IN WITNESS WHEREOF, the parties have executed this on the day and year first above written.

_____   _____
Optioner   Optionee

Rental Application and Office Forms

Some forms printed here have been used with permission from <www.mrlandlord.com> (Web site for landlords).

Rental Application
Form for Rent and Royalty Income and Expenses
Management Move-In Checklist

RENTAL APPLICATION

Date:_____ Application Fee: _____

Wants to lease: _____ Wants to move in: _____

Applicant's Name: _____ Social Security #: _____

Children's Names and Ages: _____

Present Address: _____ How long? _____

Present Landlord's Name: _____ Phone: _____

Previous Address: _____ How long? _____

Previous Landlord's Name: _____ Phone: _____

Have you ever paid rent late? _____ Why?_____

Employer: _____ Address: _____

Supervisor: _____ Job Title:_____

Length of Service: _____ Salary per week: _____

Supervisor's Phone: _____ Any arrest record? _____

Credit References   Account #   Phone #

1. _____

2. _____

3. _____

Car financed?_____ Furniture financed? _____

Name of Company: _____ Name of Company? _____

Address: _____ Address: _____

Applicant's Driver's License #: _____ State:_____

MDHA Case Worker: _____

In case of emergency: _____
                         Name   Address   Phone

I hereby authorize _____ to submit the information I have given for verification and I specifically authorize _____ to contact the employers, landlords, banks, police, for any police records and other credit references which I have listed above, for the purpose of verifying the information furnished by me in this application.

Applicant's Signature: _____

FORM FOR RENT AND ROYALTY INCOME AND EXPENSES

Kind of Property _____

Location of Property _____

TSJ ☐   State ☐

Current Year	Prior Year
_____	_____
_____	_____
_____	_____
_____	_____

Number of days property was rented at fair market value

Number of days property was used personally

Number of days property was held out for rent but not rented

What percentage of the property do you own or rent to others if not 100%?

Income and Expenses	
_____	_____
_____	_____
_____	_____
_____	_____
_____	_____
_____	_____
_____	_____
_____	_____
_____	_____
_____	_____
_____	_____
_____	_____
_____	_____
_____	_____
_____	_____
_____	_____
_____	_____
_____	_____
_____	_____
_____	_____
_____	_____
_____	_____

Rental income

Nondepletable royalty income

Other income:

Advertising

Auto and travel

Bad debts

Cleaning and maintenance

Commissions

Insurance

Legal and other professional fees

Management fees

Interest—mortgage paid to individuals

Interest—other _____

Repairs—carpentry and screens

Repairs—electrical and plumbing

Repairs—painting and decorating

Repairs—roofing

Repairs—miscellaneous

Supplies

Taxes

Utilities

Other expenses: _____

_____

Percentage Depletion Information
Property number _____

Current Year	Prior Year	Production Type

Property and Equipment

Acquisitions—Description	Date Acquired	Cost

Dispositions—Description	Date Acquired	Cost	Date Sold	Selling Price

MANAGEMENT MOVE-IN CHECKLIST

Date: _____ Tenant's Name: _____

Address: _____

- ❏ Application filled out and fee collected
- ❏ Verification filled out and fee collected
- ❏ Deposit given to reserve rental
- ❏ First month's rent collected
- ❏ Security deposit collected
- ❏ Move-in payment schedule
- ❏ Rental agreement signed and explained
- ❏ Additional agreements
- ❏ Information sheet for new tenants
- ❏ On-time payments emphasized/connection procedures
- ❏ Rental inventory sheet given and checked
- ❏ Office hours/maintenance explained
- ❏ Request/repair policies explained
- ❏ Periodic inspections discussed
- ❏ Renters Insurance suggested

INDEX

Secrets of a Millionaire Landlord

FOR SPECIAL DISCOUNTS on 20 or more copies of *Secrets of a Millionaire Landlord,* please call Dearborn Trade Special Sales at 800-621-9621, extension 4307.

Dearborn™
Trade Publishing
A **Kaplan Professional** Company